SOKAIYA

SOKAIYA

総会屋

Extortion,
Protection,
and the
Japanese
Corporation

Kenneth Szymkowiak

AN EAST GATE BOOK

M.E. Sharpe

Armonk, New York
London, England

An East Gate Book

Serialized in *The Japanese Economy: Translations and Studies*, volume 26, no. 3 and no. 4.

Cover calligraphy by Kyoko Selden.

Library of Congress Cataloging-in-Publication Data

Szymkowiak, Kenneth, 1952–
    Sokaiya : extortion, protection, and the Japanese corporation / Kenneth Szymkowiak.
        p. cm.
    Includes bibliographical references and index.
    ISBN 0-7656-0779-4 (alk. paper) — ISBN 0-7656-0780-8 (pbk. alk. paper)
        1. Extortion—Japan. 2. Commercial crimes—Japan. 3. Organized crime—Japan. 4.
    Corporations—Corrupt practices—Japan. 5. Corporate culture—Japan. I. Title.

HV6688.S99 2001
364.16'5'092—dc21   2001049150

Printed in the United States of America

Contents

Introduction

"Extortion" is a term familiar to most societies. Indeed, many people, at some point in their lives, have been perpetrators or victims of the act, in one form or another. For example, an exasperated parent will threaten, "Clean your room or you're grounded." A possessive lover will cry, "If you don't stay with me, I'll tell your [wife or husband]." The rebellious adolescent cleans his room so he can go out; the harassed lover promises to stay to avoid an ugly divorce. In such cases, it is often easier to give in than fight, meaning the perpetrators get their way—most of the time.

Extortion can take many forms. It can be obvious, like a crowbar across a knee, or subtle, like a stiletto through the ribs. Such metaphors are appropriate, because extortion is nothing more than the threat of violence supported by the victim's fear of what might happen if the demands are not met. With an utterance, the deed is done. Therefore, when someone commits extortion, on some level, it is understandable, but in almost the same instant of understanding, it is difficult to comprehend. Why would anyone allow it to take place in his or her life?

What about extortion that takes place in what is, ostensibly, public life? How are we to comprehend this? This book attempts to answer such questions. Nearly every week in Japan, acts of extortion take place involving gangsters and Japanese corporate executives. When extortion is discovered, the public's initial reaction is often shock or disgust—surely the victimized executives are somehow weak for not fighting such threats. Yet there is that small, hidden understanding lurking in the public's consciousness. The details may be unknown, but observers understand that the victim succumbed or, in a sense, "allowed" the extortion to take place. He did this because he valued something so highly in the corporation that he was willing to pay to protect it.

The *sokaiya* of Japan are professional extortionists. The one thousand or so *sokaiya* operating in Japan manipulate information they have learned about a corporation in order to extract payments from the corporation's executives. *Sokaiya* usually threaten to reveal these scandalous secrets either at the company's annual shareholder meetings or in their own publications. The executives will pay well to avoid scandal. They buy *sokaiya* silence at meetings (a violation of the Commercial Code) or purchase the entire press run of a publication. At the same time, the executives may hire *sokaiya* to defend themselves against extortionate demands and thus play one group off against another. In the end *sokaiya* are skilled in knowing what corporate "buttons" must be pushed in order to get their reward. They do not rely on weakness as much as they carefully calculate what is valuable to the corporation. For nearly a century *sokaiya* have made their demands, and the payoffs have in turn flowed to them. To understand *sokaiya*, one must remember that weakness is not the true issue. Rather, both sides of the extortionate deal involve calculating individuals who make decisions based on those calculations.

Research Notes

Research for this study in Japan was undertaken between June 1993 and December 1994. I chose the city of Kobe as my base of operations for several reasons: first, it is the headquarters of Japan's largest crime syndicate, Yamaguchi-gumi, which has strong ties to many *sokaiya* groups and individuals. Second, it is within easy commuting distance to Osaka, the major commercial center of Japan's Kansai region. Tokyo is just a few hours away by bullet train. Thus I would be in a region where many *sokaiya* are active, but perhaps less hidden, since they are not operating in the commercial heart of the nation, Tokyo.

I was already familiar with parts of Japan when I lived in Tokyo between 1983 and 1988. While there, it became obvious that the Kansai region around Osaka was generally considered a "poor relation" of Tokyo (the nation's governmental and commercial capital). However, Osaka is known as a tough business town populated by canny entrepreneurs. They have their own rough dialect, *Osaka-ben*, that immediately sets them apart from other Japanese. If there were a comparison to be made, the attitude to people from Osaka would not be dissimilar to our cultural beliefs about people hailing from Brooklyn. The city is also a major center of *sokaiya* activity, having its own stock exchange and housing a number of top Japanese enterprise headquarters. Thus I felt there might be a better chance of penetrating the *sokaiya* phenomenon through Kansai's "back door" rather than approaching through Tokyo's "main gate."

My research followed two general paths. One consisted of gathering and translating primary and secondary data materials, including journal articles, stories from local and national media, and publications produced by *sokaiya* groups and individuals who privately publish materials for dissemination to others interested in *sokaiya*. These latter persons were usually corporate managers or lawyers whose livelihood involves working for corporations as *sokaiya* monitors or handlers. Many of these resources were found in libraries, but others, especially those items produced by *sokaiya*, were provided by persons who passed them on with the condition that they remain anonymous. I have respected this condition throughout the book for reasons of their safety. They made it very clear that they feared cooperation with me could be used against them and that they or their families risked physical harm if their cooperation with me became known.

The second research path involved a series of interviews with individuals familiar with the *sokaiya* phenomenon and related issues. These sources included corporate managers who deal or have dealt with *sokaiya* in the course of their work, police officials charged with investigating and controlling *sokaiya*, lawyers involved in anti-organized-crime activities, members of organized-crime syndicates, and *sokaiya* themselves.

The interview process involved a kind of "filtration." Those to be interviewed always asked—indirectly, with mild probing—how sincerely interested I was in the subject, and attempted to ascertain how knowledgeable I was. Consequently, our first meetings revolved largely around me and seldom provided much useful data about my subject. The sources would gauge my sincerity and knowledge and, in turn, would establish their own expertise and lay the ground rules for the discussion.

However, in some cases the promised interviews never materialized. I found two reasons for this. First, as interviews with *sokaiya* were arranged, they would often ask for a prepared set of questions. On one occasion, the interview was called off because the questions were too general; on another occasion, no interview took place, because the same questions submitted in the previous instance were deemed too specific.

The second reason for my failure to gain what I consider a sufficient number of interviews for my hoped-for goals was, simply, poor timing and bad luck, although the latter might seem a bit gruesome to most readers. Interviewing began in the fall of 1993, with the number of interviews increasing from one every two or three weeks to several per week. Sometimes they were simply intermediary talks, as described above, and I sometimes sensed I was being passed up the line to higher and higher levels of informants. Then, in late February 1994, a director of the Fuji Photo Film Corporation was murdered outside his Tokyo home, and all interviews abruptly ended.

The director (I will discuss his murder later in the book) oversaw the operation of the company's shareholder meetings and was assigned the task of implementing a policy that cut or ended payoffs to *sokaiya*. One *sokaiya* group based in Osaka was particularly outraged by this new policy and is widely believed to be responsible for the director's death— although they might not have done the act themselves, but instead "contracted" it out.

The effect of his murder on my research was that talkative sources turned silent. I was warned to be careful about my own safety. One lawyer who has ongoing contacts with *sokaiya* suggested I be careful on train and subway platforms.

Another lawyer with similar connections was constantly concerned that I avoid any contact with him at his office lest I run into the "wrong" people.

The "paranoia" (and melodrama) was palpable, heightened for me by unannounced visits to my apartment by a member of an organized-crime group. While always bearing gifts and taking time for a cup of coffee, he would ask repeatedly if I intended to follow through on my research project. When told that the project was moving along as planned, he would find an excuse to leave quickly, his business apparently finished.

This atmosphere of fear and suspicion ran its course and faded by the end of the summer of 1994. Everything seemed back on track until a second executive, this time a branch manager for Sumitomo Bank, was killed outside his apartment in Nagoya. Although this incident apparently had no direct connection to *sokaiya* and was largely believed to be part of a dispute involving bad loans, the effect was the same as before: my carefully constructed system of informants collapsed. Let me be clear: the violence and threats of violence, the warnings and fear were not a product of my own research. As I will show, they represent a particularly violent period of *sokaiya*-corporate relations as companies reduced or eliminated payoffs due to the post-bubble-economy recession in the early 1990s.

In the end, however, my research in Japan was fruitful and important, allowing me to add some measure of depth to the secondary resource material, some of which was quite dated but nonetheless still helpful. On another level, however, I was introduced to something perhaps just as important: what Italians who monitor the Mafia call the "interpretation of signs."

In his book, *Excellent Cadavers*, which chronicles the 1992 assassinations of Mafia prosecutors Giovanni Falcone and Paolo Borsellino, author Alexander Stille writes:

> Murders are carried out not only to eliminate a dangerous adversary but to make a clear, unequivocal statement when more subtle forms of communication have been ignored. "Everything is a message, everything is full of meaning in the world of Cosa Nostra, no detail is too small to be overlooked," Falcone wrote in an autobiographical memoir. . . . "[T]he *mafioso* communicates indirectly through actions, gestures and silences." "The interpretation of signs," Falcone added, "is one of the principal activities of a 'man of honor' [a *mafioso*] and consequently of the mafia-prosecutor." (Stille 1995, 6–7)

The similarity of the above passage to the words of one source who worked for a Kansai corporation as a *sokaiya* handler (making payoffs, negotiating, acting as intermediary, etc.) is striking. As part of his regular job the source was expected to monitor and interpret the actions of *sokaiya*, and, he said, "Everything a *sokaiya* does has meaning."

Content

Chapter 1 of this book introduces the *sokaiya* phenomenon by indirectly beginning to answer some significant questions: How much importance do *sokaiya* have in the Japanese corporate system? How widespread are they? Why are *sokaiya* feared?

The tags, or labels, of *sokaiya* are laid out in chapter 1; they describe the activities of *sokaiya* and provide clues as to how *sokaiya* are ranked by corporate managers. In turn, this ranking determines how large a payoff a *sokaiya* will receive. While little is known about present-day payoffs to *sokaiya*, the payments made prior to Commercial Code reform in 1982 are well known and give some idea of the breadth of the phenomenon. The *sokaiya*'s deep entrenchment in the Japanese corporate system is revealed by the rich terminology used to describe them and their actions. This terminology is linked to concrete actions by individuals, which result in concrete effects that in turn reinforce the *sokaiya*-corporate relationship.

Chapter 2 examines the history of *sokaiya* as far as we can determine it from primary and secondary resources. It reveals the sociocultural basis for *sokaiya* established in pre–Meiji era Japan. Comparisons are made between Japan and the existence of what I term informal private-security groups in other nations, particularly the United States, Great Britain, and Italy. Such groups are deemed informal when compared to the police or other security groups formally sanctioned or regulated by the Japanese state through legal measures.

The history carries through into the decades after World War II. Although the Allied Occupation instilled a number of reforms into the corporate legal system, *sokaiya* remain embedded and were capable of manipulating new rules and resources for their benefit. I will examine key incidents that demonstrate this capability. I will also explore incidents that on the surface seem to have no connection with Japanese corporations, especially the changing relations between the nation's dominant political force and the *yakuza*. As an informal private-security group, the *yakuza* were once considered a shadow ally in protecting the conservative government from radical and progressive forces. However, that changed over time, and the *yakuza* and their allies within the radical right came to be viewed as another threat. Crackdowns by the formal police forces helped drive some *yakuza* into *sokaiya* rackets, thus increasing pressure on corporations.

Although few observers were prescient enough to see it at the time, events within and without the *sokaiya* system began to converge in the late 1960s and early 1970s, and these events are discussed in chapter 3. Direct confrontations with pollution victims—most notably those of the Minamata mercury poisoning—and anti–Vietnam War peace activists began to heat up. Corporations targeted by these groups in turn used trusted *sokaiya*, *yakuza*, and members of the radical right to suppress the protesters. Such conflicts presented Japanese government leaders with a dilemma that they attempted to resolve through legislative reform. In addition, the police and corporations acted to form the first anti-*sokaiya* protection associations designed to limit *sokaiya* activity. The effects of these associations and how corporate executives maneuvered through them to maintain *sokaiya* contacts are also examined in chapter 3.

Chapter 4 details the process of reform of the Commercial Code. The case of legal reform covered is unusual in Japan in that the debate among government bureaucrats, legal scholars, and corporate leaders was comparatively open to the public, mainly through the print media of legal journals. Among the data examined are responses to a questionnaire formulated by the code-reform subcommittee and distributed to approximately fifty organizations seeking their opinions on a variety of topics, including social responsibility of the corporation (reflecting concerns about the antipollution and antiwar protests), how to reinvigorate the shareholder meeting, and the need for *sokaiya*.

The Commercial Code was eventually reformed in 1982. Chapter 5 explores the effects of the reform up to the present. One part of the code made the use of corporate funds to pay for *sokaiya* services an illegal act. It was designed to break the financial link between corporations and *sokaiya*—but did the reform have the desired effect? What effects did it have? How did corporate managers and *sokaiya* maintain their links and adapt?

Chapter 6 attempts to answer the next obvious questions: Why are payoffs made? What makes *sokaiya* so powerful? What are the cultural rules and resources available to them and how do they use them? This chapter includes a discussion of the concept of "face" and how it is used by *sokaiya* and maintained by managers. In order to do this, I will explore in detail a transcript of one stormy shareholder meeting of a major clothing manufacturer in Japan. I will show not only what tactics the *sokaiya* used to disrupt the meeting, but how the harassed chairman of the meeting and other executives dealt with these tactics.

Chapter 7 examines two more significant events directly affecting the *sokaiya* phenomenon. First was the passage of the Violent Group Countermeasures Law (*Boryokudan Taisaku-ho*), which was aimed at *sokaiya* and other violent groups using extortion as a means to interfere in disputes that could be resolved by legal means—everything from shareholder grievances to traffic-accident settlements. The law tightened the social screws on some *sokaiya* and provided corporations desiring to end links with *sokaiya* a legal resource to take action through police cooperation.

The second significant event covered in this chapter was the bursting of the so-called bubble economy in the late 1980s and early 1990s, just as the anti–organized-crime law came on the books. The resulting recession caused corporations to review expenditures, decrease hiring, and—significantly for *sokaiya*—limit payments for their services or stop them altogether. This corporate belt-tightening led to a major increase in violent attacks against corporate executives, including the murders of three corporate managers, one directly linked to *sokaiya*.

Broadly speaking, my examination of *sokaiya* is not merely an exercise in the analysis of extortion, although this is important. Of far more interest sociologically is what the *sokaiya* phenomenon reveals about the Japanese corporate system and society in general. Chapter 8 draws the many threads discussed in the previous chapters together into a tapestry of events describing a capitalist system populated by agents obsessed with maintaining control through the use of any rule or resource available.

SOKAIYA

総会屋

1

Reconstructing *Sokaiya*

On February 28, 1994, Juntaro Suzuki, a sixty-one-year-old managing director of Fuji Photo Film Corporation was stabbed to death on the doorstep of his home.

Suzuki and his wife, Michiko, lived in a modest home on a narrow side street in Tokyo's Setagaya Ward, a fashionable residential area near the shallow Tamagawa, the river that serves as the border between Tokyo and the industrial city of Kawasaki. Mrs. Suzuki was taping a television program for her son, who was on an overseas trip. The doorbell rang and Mr. Suzuki answered the door using an intercom. The man at the door said his car had hit part of the wall surrounding Suzuki's home. He asked if someone could come out to inspect the damage.

Suzuki agreed and went out. Neighbors said later that there was some brief shouting, perhaps even a few cries for help. Mrs. Suzuki said that all she heard was her husband weakly calling "Mama" when she found him on the step, dying from wounds on his head, legs, and arms. According to police reports, the wounds were consistent in shape with those made by a Japanese sword. The nature of the wounds gave rise to the suspicion that Suzuki was a victim of right-wing terrorism. Japan's radical right is well known for its attacks against corporations and their executives. The Japanese sword is one of their favorite weapons, although the right wing is also known to use Molotov cocktails and the occasional firearm to shoot into a vacant home or office. But radical-right involvement became less and less a possibility as Suzuki's encounters with extortionists became increasingly known. The details of the case pointed toward sokaiya.[1]

Sokaiya are a relatively unknown phenomenon in the West. Their acts of extortion against Japanese corporations are seldom reported by Western media; their work as an informal private-security force for other corporations is mentioned even less often. Nonetheless they meet the requirements of an organized-crime group as described by Kenney and Finckenauer (1995) in their review of definitions of organized crime. *Sokaiya* groups are hierarchical, self-perpetuating, engage in conspiratorial acts, provide illegal services as well as legal services in an illegal manner, are linked with corrupt public officials who cooperate with them and maintain a layer of immunity for their acts, and, finally, use violence or the threat of violence to facilitate their criminal activities (Kennedy and Finckenauer 1995, 25–28). So how do they fit inside Japanese organized crime?

In the constellation of groups comprising Japanese organized crime, *sokaiya* certainly are less well known than the *yakuza*, who make up the more traditional branch of syndicate crime. The *yakuza* can trace their existence back hundreds of years. Some *yakuza* are also *sokaiya*, but not all *sokaiya* are *yakuza*—that is, many *sokaiya* who operate in the subculture of organized crime in Japan do not participate in the various traditions, fictive kinship rites, and relationships required of a *yakuza* to become what an American mafioso might call a "made" member (Iwai 1974). In the *yakuza*, one does not "make his bones" through the murder of another. Instead, membership in a group is formally accomplished through the acceptance of allegiance to a more senior member of the organization.

Unlike the *yakuza*, *sokaiya* are a rather modern development in Japan's organized-crime subculture, growing out of a particular set of circumstances present in late-nineteenth-century Japan and then adapting as those circumstances changed up to the present. *Sokaiya* would not find it necessary to develop or participate in the traditional culture- and history-bound rites of *yakuza* such as finger cutting, tattooing, or drinking sake from the same cup as their leader. *Sokaiya* are part of a distinctly foreign-based development in modern Japanese history—the development of capitalism during the modernization of the Japanese state following hundreds of years of extremely controlled exposure to the West and other foreign influences. The *yakuza* existed long before capitalism was ever known. *Sokaiya*, on the other hand, could not exist without modern capitalism and the joint-stock corporation in Japan.

Why is this so? Because *sokaiya* are usually defined as persons who disrupt shareholder meetings by asking questions or by engaging in violent acts against other shareholders or corporate managers. Consequently, corporate managers occasionally make payoffs to *sokaiya* to prevent such disturbances. Such services are merely part of an array of "favors" provided by *sokaiya* to managers willing to hire them. These services include suppressing other *sokaiya* or even regular shareholders bold enough to ask questions at shareholder meetings. So, without the corporation and the annual shareholder meeting required by the Japanese Commercial Code, *sokaiya* could not exist.

However, such a definition misses at least part of the point regarding *sokaiya*. They are sometimes extortionists, sometimes mercenaries—who are also Japanese. In other words, they lead lives dominated by the cultural and historical traditions of the Japanese people created over thousands of years. *Sokaiya* clearly understand, perhaps sometimes at an intuitive level, how they and others go about being Japanese.

This point is obvious enough that it might be ignored, but it does help answer the questions asked about *sokaiya*: What is peculiar to Japanese corporations that provides a place for *sokaiya*? Why are Japanese corporations, which have an image of great power on national and international levels, unable to eliminate *sokaiya* from the corporate system? Why are there no American or German *sokaiya* or, for that matter, *sokaiya* in any other modern capitalist nation?

The answer is simple: There are elements of Japanese culture, history, language, and even gesture that lend themselves to abuse through extortion, intimidation, domination, and control. Such elements either do not exist in other cultures, or the reactions to them are quite different from those that a Japanese person might have. Certainly the concepts of the corporation and capitalism could exist in Japan without *sokaiya*. But the elements of Japanese society that affect how the Japanese think about themselves, about others, and how they interact are also intrinsic parts of the capitalist system in Japan.

Before proceeding further, we need a better understanding of *sokaiya* and those with whom they most often interact—usually corporate managers and the police.

In the West, criminal and unethical activities are not always well documented. Often, newspaper articles or television reports are strained through layers of bias. Different people interpret events differently, even if the very same event is witnessed by all. As a result, the interpretation of those events can differ over time and depending on who provides the interpretation.

For example, police and prosecutors ask one set of questions to see if an action fits within the elements of a crime; journalists ask another set to see if an action makes a newsworthy story. The intent of their questions is inherently dissimilar; hence the answers and how they are processed are different. The reconstruction of events "are constructions, rather than reflections, of reality" (Ferrel and Sanders 1995, 308). If criminality is involved, witnesses give careful thought to how much knowledge they want to reveal. Some people, perhaps, cannot "remember"; others did not "see." Still others simply do not "know" anything. Reactions to such situations are no different in Japan: people are reluctant to talk about crime or scandal when it is close to them. This begs the question: How does one uncover what could be the "truth" about *sokaiya* who are so well hidden and protected in the Japanese system?

One answer lies in how the Japanese themselves describe *sokaiya*. The Japanese language is studded with colorful labels that, once analyzed, help broaden our understanding of *sokaiya*, just as when someone is declared part of the mafia, depending on one's experience, varying images are raised in the mind. But one must get beyond image to reach some reconstruction of reality.

The labels the Japanese give to *sokaiya* are not only colorful, but practical as well, revealing that the *sokaiya* profession, far from being simply an obscure form of organized crime, is a field with clearly defined divisions of labor and paths of advancement. Such labels also help company managers determine how to deal with individual *sokaiya*.

Origin of the Term *Sokaiya*

The term *sokaiya* is derived from the combination of the word *sokai,* which means "general meeting"—in this case, the general meeting of company shareholders. Other groups such as religious organizations may hold general meetings, but *sokaiya* are not involved. The suffix *ya* refers to a person engaged in the business described by the root word. Hence, *sokaiya* refers to someone involved in the business of general shareholder meetings.

Not surprisingly, this means very little to the average Westerner. To such an individual, the given meaning might indicate that the *sokaiya* is in charge of running a meeting, ensuring that the chairs are arranged, that water and glasses are set out for the board of directors, and so on. To the average Japanese, however, *sokaiya* has decidedly negative connotations.

I learned this very early in my fieldwork. Just after arriving in Japan, I attended a party at the U.S. Embassy compound in Tokyo for new Fulbright-grant recipients. A Japanese colleague, knowing my intended topic of research, was eager to introduce me to a man who, he said, was knowledgeable about *sokaiya* since he had worked for many years as a director of a major corporation. After introductions, the former director inquired as to what I would be researching. Once he understood clearly that I was studying *sokaiya*, he abruptly turned and walked away without another word, making sure for the rest of the evening that he kept his distance and that he was protected from me by several of his friends.

When I recounted this incident to another Japanese colleague who has worked as a *sokaiya* "watcher" for decades, he explained, with some amusement, that the topic of *sokaiya* is distasteful, and certainly not something mentioned in polite company—equivalent to making scatological remarks during a formal dinner. In fact, the word *sokaiya* has become so weighted with negative images that even *sokaiya* prefer that others do not use it and have attempted to construct new terms to describe themselves.

Sokaiya, corporate managers in charge of dealing with *sokaiya*, and others familiar with the phenomenon might refer to *sokaiya* as *kabunushi undo-ka* ("shareholder activists"), but they are far more likely to describe them as *tokushu kabunushi* or "special shareholders" (Inoue 1966, 58). Before the Japanese Commercial Code was changed in 1982 to eliminate or at least control *sokaiya*, *Shoji homu*, a respected legal journal, used the term *sokaiya* to identify *sokaiya* in its annual survey of corporations and shareholder meetings.[2] After the 1982 reform, when *sokaiya* payoffs became illegal, the editors used the term *kodo ma-ku kabunushi* (literally, "shareholders who are marked as active" or "marked shareholders"). The term usually refers to *sokaiya*, but it might also include real shareholder activists not interested in payoffs but in changing company policy. Or it could be a label for greenmailer groups (otherwise known as *shite* groups). Greenmailers in Japan, as in the rest of the world, purchase shares of a company in order to force the company to repurchase the shares at an inflated price (see Kester 1991, 245–62, and Isaacs and Ejiri 1990, 113–14, for descriptions of such Japanese groups and explanations of their activities). One source revealed that *kodo ma-ku kabunushi* was probably coined to allow companies to claim some sort of contact with *sokaiya* without actually admitting such contacts, as mingling with *sokaiya* usually implies some sort of illegal transaction is taking place and may attract unwanted attention from authorities.

It is not known who first coined the term *sokaiya*. One colorful suggestion comes from Shoichi Taniguchi, a prominent *sokaiya* active in the late 1970s, who published a book about his profession. He wrote that the label gained popular usage in the early twentieth century through the efforts of Tokyo geisha, who described their customers by the business in which the men were engaged. Those in the securities industry were called *kabuya-san* (*kabu* meaning "share of corporate stock"; *ya* meaning "one in the business of"; and the general honorific *san*), or "Mr. Stockbroker." Those in the banking profession were called *ginkoya-san* (*ginko* meaning "bank"), or "Mr. Banker." The geisha's use of the sobriquet *sokaiya-san* gave these patrons a sense of belonging to a profession at least equal to those who sold stocks or worked for banks (Taniguchi 1980, 539).[3]

There are other, more specific labels delineating types of *sokaiya* as well as the kind of action they perform. These labels, discussed below, show a complex working system—at least as complex as those used to describe types of attorneys (tax attorneys or public defenders, for example) or doctors (obstetricians, internists, etc.).

Descriptive Tags

Sokaiya generally fall into two main categories, depending on what they do: *yato sokaiya* and *yoto sokaiya*. The word *yato* is used to describe an opposing political party or particular member of that party. In the case of *sokaiya*, however, "yato" designates those persons working against a particular corporation at a shareholder meeting. The word *yoto* most often means a ruling political party, but for *sokaiya* it defines a person working on behalf of the corporation's agenda at a meeting.

> Before World War II it was the general practice of a number of public companies to offer money and other economic benefits

to a limited number of "specialists" to ensure that they attended general meetings for the purpose of encouraging orderly proceedings and to support company management.

These specialists became known as *yoto sokaiya* . . . Companies began to recognise that the attendance of well-established specialists could often guarantee that there would be no disruption to the meeting, as they used violence and other unlawful means of influence to ensure the non-attendance of shareholders who held opinions contrary to those of management. (Isaacs and Ejiri 1990, 124)

A *sokaiya* is not tagged with these descriptive terms for the length of his career. He may be called a *yato sokaiya* one day and a *yoto sokaiya* the next, moving between the two at will or as necessary. But the term *yoto sokaiya* has a deeper meaning, suggesting an alliance with a company that resembles a relationship between a consultant (the *sokaiya*) and a client (the corporation). As will be shown below, such "consultant" work can become a very powerful informal position within a corporation.

In addition to the above two main designations, there are at least eight general subdesignations describing what work a *sokaiya* may perform on a day-to-day basis. The subdesignations partially reveal the rank of the *sokaiya* and help corporate managers determine how much money he should receive either as a payoff or for services rendered.

Bunkatsuya (Dividers)

Before the 1982 Commercial Code reform, many *sokaiya* could jump-start their careers by becoming *bunkatsuya*. The *sokaiya* would buy a hundred shares of a company, and, under normal circumstances, a single stock certificate showing ownership of a hundred shares would be issued by the company. The *sokaiya* then would demand that a separate certificate be issued for each share. Once this was done, he would return to the corporation and announce that the shares were not actually his any longer but that he was acting as representative for a hundred individual stockholders. He then would demand that new certificates be filled out with the proper name of each owner. The company then would be required to contact each shareholder on the *sokaiya*'s ownership list to determine if, indeed, he was acting as the individual's agent. Finally, the company would issue a number of documents indicating the transfer and assignment of the single share to the new individual.

Even one *bunkatsuya* could cause so much paperwork to be produced by an office that it could jam normal operations for days. Companies thus might find it far easier to try to convince the *bunkatsuya* to retain the hundred shares in his own name by offering him a sum of money for his troubles. However, even were he to accept the bribe, the *sokaiya* could decide the next day that the arrangement was too much trouble and return to the company demanding the division of the stock, thus repeating the process and getting a new payoff. If he was industrious, he would use part of his payoff money to purchase shares in another company and begin the process there as well.

Such incidents can be a real financial drain on a corporation. The late 1970s saw a dramatic increase in the *sokaiya* population (from around six hundred in 1970 to nearly six thousand by 1979), and many of these men were earning money through *bunkatsuya* operations.

> Companies must send to each shareholder six or more different kinds of documents prior to a shareholder meeting. . . . This led

one observer to note: "In one year a company may pay out five yen per share in dividends while spending 2,000 yen per shareholder. There is no way to explain this imbalance." . . . [E]ach year it is estimated companies spend an average 840 million yen on shareholder management fees. For an average company this represents 0.7 percent of total capital, 2.8 percent of taxable profit or 7.2 percent of dividends. ("Sokaiya no mitsuida kigyo 240–sha risuto" 1978: 120.)

The key for the *bunkatsuya* is to use his payoffs to purchase shares from as many companies as possible. As he expands his holdings, his name becomes known in the business community, thus ensuring a continuing and expanding income. However, the *bunkatsuya*'s job was made slightly more difficult when, just prior to the 1982 code reform, securities companies independently decided to sell shares in lots of one thousand rather than smaller odd lots.

Banzaiya (Supporters)

Banzaiya are *sokaiya* who push through a company's agenda at a meeting by shouting *Igi nashi* ("No objections"). They also show up at corporate events such as anniversary celebrations of a company's founding and act as well-wishers, shouting "Banzai!" at appropriate moments. In return for this "service," they expect to receive a small honorarium. These *sokaiya* are sometimes also known as *shinkoya*, or "advancers."

Sokai Arashi (General Meeting Storm Makers)

These *sokaiya* engage in disruptive, often violent activities at shareholder meetings. In the 1960s, the Japanese courts (the cases will be reviewed later) attempted to draw a distinction between *sokaiya* and *sokai arashi*. Lawyers argued—and a lower court agreed—that the *sokaiya* were useful, even helpful fixtures in a shareholder meeting, while *sokai arashi* were merely disruptive. A higher court struck down the lower court's finding, however, arguing that, given the changeable nature of *sokaiya* work (*yato* and *yoto*), such a distinction could not be drawn—in other words, a *sokaiya* is a *sokaiya* is a *sokaiya*.

Chukaiya (Intermediaries)

These are *sokaiya* who offer to act as go-betweens, sometimes working in collusion with *sokai arashi*. *Chukaiya* will offer their services to management as arbitrators to placate disruptive *sokai arashi*—the implicit threat being that if their services are not retained, the company will face further problems. Such activities might take place before or during the meeting. At times, if *sokaiya* are harassing a particular company for an extended period, management might request the services of a *chukaiya* to mediate the dispute.

Boeiya (Defenders)

Boeiya are hired to form, in a very literal sense, a defensive line in front of the chairman and the board in order to fend off any violent attacks against the board. Experienced *boeiya* are also known to be quite familiar with the Commercial Code and are able to add their voices to debates, thereby overwhelming those attacking the company. At times a corporation will send in its own employees to bolster this front line. Some managers of shareholder meetings ensure physical protection by filling the first and second rows of seats at a meeting with *boeiya* and employees.

Kogekiya (Attackers)

Although they are disruptive, *kogekiya* are slightly different from *sokai arashi* in that they are less prone to violence, preferring to disrupt the meeting with prolonged questioning and debate on a variety of topics.

Enshutsuya (Producers)

Enshutsuya are expected to ensure that meetings are conducted without incident. These men are often high-ranking *sokaiya* (see below) who bring a large group of followers with them to meetings.

Enkaiya (Adjourners)

Although the name implies that these men attempt to bring meetings to a close, in fact they specialize in prolonging meetings by blocking the attempts of *sokaiya* who are trying to end them quickly.

The above subdesignations indicate a career system in which everyone has a place, a job to perform, and a role to play—and all players understand this. There are no misunderstandings about what is going on and who is taking part. Just as important, however, is the fact that *sokaiya* and others use these very tags to gauge their own career status and that of others. According to Taniguchi, *sokaiya* such as *bunkatsuya* and *banzaiya* are largely beginners, unimpressive, and considered on the fringe of the *sokaiya* world. They seldom have a following, and perform their work using a small office with a single phone. They enjoy, Taniguchi wrote, "an existence which was otherwise not noteworthy" (Taniguchi 1980, 540–41).

Other *sokaiya* may carry more weight, and some become important characters in the *sokaiya* field. This is more easily determined by the ranks others give them but which they are very concerned about.

Rankings and Payoffs

Corporate managers use a ranking system to determine how much money will be paid to *sokaiya*. The ranks range from "A" to "E," with "A" denoting the highest-ranking and most powerful *sokaiya*. According to management insiders, the ranks are not arbitrary; rather, they are applied to individuals after managers from different companies hold discussions about them. Informal files kept by these managers add to the information used to determine the rank importance of a *sokaiya*. One source displayed a large, meticulously cross-referenced paper and electronic database of individual *sokaiya*. The database included reports of each *sokaiya*'s activities over the years. Whenever a call came from a colleague, this manager could pinpoint the actions of a particular *sokaiya*, assess the strengths and weaknesses of the man, identify his boss, allies, and any underlings, and estimate how much he would need for a payoff.

In general, the rankings indicate the following: an "A"-class rank belongs to *sokaiya* who usually side with a company, own shares in hundreds of corporations, and have long experience in meeting the needs of managers in and out of the shareholder meeting. They become close associates of management and constantly search for information that may prove useful in their work with companies. These men will also be called upon by management to plan strategies for upcoming shareholder meetings designed to block or nullify attacks from other *sokaiya* groups.

"A"-class *sokaiya* are often called *omono sokaiya* (major *sokaiya*). According to one source, at least one *omono sokaiya* operating mainly in the area around Osaka was so powerful as well as knowledgeable that companies would consult with him before deciding who would become their next president. If the *omono sokaiya* was aware of some otherwise hidden scandal involving the candidate, he could save the company from potential harm. The source added that this practice is not unusual and that he knows of several men rejected for corporate presidencies because of career or personal problems that could be used against a company by other *sokaiya*.

"B"-class *sokaiya* may work for or against a company (*yato* or *yoto*). They usually attempt to enter the "A"-class rank and become incensed when management rejects their "help." When they are rejected, they will either maintain their anticompany position until the firm gives in or they will launch a campaign to ingratiate themselves with a company until it bestows a consultant status on them.

"C"-class *sokaiya* are the rank-and-file members of *sokaiya* groups and are followers of "A"- and "B"-class *sokaiya*. They more often follow orders from above than issue them to underlings, but they are highly valued for their loyalty to their individual leader. They may have their own small group of two or three men to train, but their access to useful information is far more limited than that of "B"- or "A"-class *sokaiya*.

"D"-class *sokaiya* are unlikely to be leaders of even small organizations. They are experienced with and know how to run or disrupt a meeting, but they are still considered in the learning stages and not ready to form an effective group. Many are involved in developing specialties that can boost their image among other *sokaiya*. For example, they might develop a highly refined understanding of commercial law or the ability to use computers in analyzing or discovering information about corporations. They often associate with *sokaiya* of the same rank or take on newcomers who may be looking for a *sempai* (senior) as an ally.

"E"-class *sokaiya* are most often frontline troops within a *sokaiya* group. They are involved in the fighting, on either side, if it breaks out in a meeting. They act only at the direction of superiors and are not expected to take any initiative, but they are expected to hold the opinions of their leaders.

Police Terminology

Although corporate managers may find the ranking system useful, the Japanese police are far less concerned about *sokaiya* ranks. Hence, their own labels are more limited, albeit just as pragmatic. Before the 1982 Commercial Code reform, the term *sokaiya* was universally applied to anyone receiving payoffs in exchange for exercising or not exercising their rights as shareholders. After the reform, the word *sokaiya* referred only to those individuals who held more than a thousand shares of a company's stock—due to the minimum-unit-stock rule (discussed later) giving the right to vote, ask questions at shareholder meetings, and so on, only to those who hold a minimum unit of a thousand shares.

The change in shareholder status resulted in police reporting a dramatic drop in the number of *sokaiya* after the reform: from 6,783 in 1982 to 1,682 in 1983. And yet, some confusion as to what exactly "made" a *sokaiya* remained, as evidenced in an interview with a police official who consistently used the precode reform definition of *sokaiya*, although he was aware that such usage was incorrect in the legal sense. He attempted to explain that those persons who did not meet the minimum-unit requirement and who did not drop out of the field completely were retagged *kaisha-goro* or *sokai-goro*. (The suffix "goro" is an abbreviated form of the word *gorotsuki,* or "ruffian.")

Thus, among the police, *kaisha-goro*, are "company ruffians" (*kaisha* meaning "company") who cause trouble for a firm outside the boundaries of the annual shareholder meeting. Since they do not own the required shares to take any action within the meeting hall, they might instead attack or confront executives at their homes or invade an office, breaking furniture and threatening employees until the manager pays them to leave. In such cases, it is not unusual for ultrarightists to be involved in the harassment, and I will discuss in detail the links between the ultraright, the *yakuza*, and *sokaiya* below. The acts of the *kaisha-goro* are merely one phase in an extortion campaign that, alone, is not very significant. However, when acts *outside* the company's shareholder meeting are combined with intimidation *during* a meeting, management's will to resist can falter or collapse. There is just too much pressure.

Sokai-goro are those who commit violent acts at shareholder meetings even though they do not own the minimum unit of stock to qualify for full rights as a shareholder. Their actions often involve direct verbal or physical attacks on the chairman or other members of the board, or against targeted shareholders, including other *sokaiya*. Although they are not allowed to speak or ask questions at meetings, they will raise their voices in protest or support at the discretion of their leader. They are most dangerous, however, when involved in assaults on management. If managers do not have a strong line of *boeiya* for protection, some *sokai-goro* will attempt to attack.

Two other types of "ruffians" exist in police parlance and are linked to the *sokaiya* world: *shimbun-goro* (newspaper ruffians) and *zasshi-goro* (magazine ruffians). These individuals publish small newspapers and magazines (so-called *mini-comi*) containing unflattering articles about a particular company. Occasionally the targeted company may be given the option of buying up the entire pressrun at a premium price to keep the publication from circulating. At other times, companies are asked to purchase subscriptions or advertising in the publications—with the implicit threat that refusal could lead to trouble later. Rondan Doyu-kai, the large *sokaiya* group mentioned before, produces a full-color tabloid highlighting group activities, including promotions, new arrivals to the group, and various trivial items. One issue contained a full page of photographs of the group's participation in a local festival in which they carried a portable shrine through the streets. During an interview, another *sokaiya* displayed a newsletter that included charts and graphs, insisting that it contained information companies needed and relied on him to get. It was clear, however, that the charts and graphs were taken directly out of business magazines and journals and redrawn on a personal computer. His discussion of the newsletter ended when I pointed out that a number of articles he wrote came from just-published business magazines.

The Japanese radical right uses the same tactic to raise or extort funding from corporations. Kunio Suzuki, a notable leader in Japan's modern radical right wing, has written of the difficulties faced by right-wingers in raising money from companies. Groups often are tempted into extortion, he explained, because managers refuse to purchase a group's publication or make a donation to the cause. So, he concludes, it is not always by choice that individuals end up as *shimbun-goro* or *zasshi-goro* (Suzuki 1993, 127–38).

Company managers may buy such magazines or newspapers as they contain useful articles, such as details about a competitor's personnel problems or management gaffes. However, the post-bubble-economy recession of the 1990s made it difficult to make payments for all the publications offered, and managers claim either to have reduced payments across the board or to reject editions on a case-by-case basis. Sometimes, however, if trouble appears imminent, they will buy simply to avoid it.

Beyond those discussed above, police also sometimes identify *sokaiya* as either *uyoku sokaiya* (right-wing) or *boryokudan sokaiya* or sometimes *yakuza sokaiya* (the latter two indicating direct links to traditional organized criminal groups). *Uyoku-sokaiya* assume the cover of a radical-right-wing political group in order to carry out their operations against companies. *Yakuza-sokaiya* work as *sokaiya*, but are also members of an organized-crime group. Before Commercial Code reform, an estimated 29.66 percent of the *sokaiya* population were members of organized-crime groups. As of this writing, that number has dropped to below 10 percent. The use of the *yakuza* front has been particularly profitable.

> According to one banker in charge of dealing with *sokaiya*: "It's a fact that there are more and more *sokaiya* who, just by looking at them, you know they are *yakuza*. A company has a certain amount of money to use for *sokaiya* payoffs and those in charge of dealing with *sokaiya* work day and night to see that it's well used. But the *sokaiya* from *yakuza* groups are frightening and inevitably the money flows to them." ("Zoka suru Boryoku-sokaiya no gokuhi risuto o hatsukokai" 1978, 84)

Sokaiya Characteristics

The statistical and descriptive information in this section is based on a document entitled *Tanto-sha hikkei* (Manager's Manual). The 298-page document consists largely of a detailed list of *sokaiya* active in Japan. No publisher is mentioned in the pages of the document. In a brief message to users, the compiler or compilers report that the information is based on individual interviews, memos, and surveys with corporate executives and those who have contact with *sokaiya* group members. It covers the years 1985 and 1986. Later editions are also available but I was unable to obtain them.

The manual contains a listing of 805 *sokaiya*—793 active, eleven deceased, and one person known to be retired. According to the National Police Agency, there were some 1,200 *sokaiya* known to be active in Japan during those years, thus this document contains information on 66.8 percent of the estimated *sokaiya* population. This permits some generalizations about the overall *sokaiya* population based on biographical and other information found in the volume, especially brief sketches of each *sokaiya*.

These sketches often include such information as date and place of birth, group affiliation if any, whether the individual works with management, against management, or on both sides, any expertise (law, accounting, etc.), university attended, and details. They also include a list of company shareholder meetings where the individual spoke out or otherwise disrupted the meeting in 1985 or 1986.

Of the 793 active sokaiya, 488 (61.53 percent) were affiliated with groups. The remaining 305 either operated independently or would be hired on periodically to bolster a group's manpower. There were 195 groups known to be operating, though few are very large. The overwhelming majority (179 or 91.79 percent) of the groups numbered no more than five members. Fifteen groups counted between six and twenty members. Only Rondan Doyu-kai, the largest *sokaiya* group in Japan, surpassed these totals with thirty-nine members.

Some groups carry the name of the group leader as the group name, such as the "Eiji Shimazaki Family" and the "Hamamoto Seiji Group." This is similar to mainstream organized-crime groups that take on the name of the leader.

Other groups pass themselves off as newspaper-publishing companies such as *Showa nichinichi shimbun* (Showa Daily Newspaper) and *Shin Osaka shimbun* (New Osaka Newspaper), advertising companies like Keizai Kokokusha (Economic Advertising Company), research organizations such as Kigyo Kenkyujo (Enterprise Research Center), and political organizations whose names express ultranationalist persuasions such as Dai-Nippon Kamikaze Doshi-Kai (Great Japan Kamikaze Brotherhood) and Dai-Nippon Issei-kai (Great Japan General Association). Some individuals are also identified as members of *yakuza* organizations.

Some 51.45 percent of the cases included a date of birth. More than half (57.7 percent) were born between 1930 and 1949. Thus, many *sokaiya* active in the postwar era came of age following the war and spent their early years involved in the antipollution and antiwar protests.

The place of birth of 423 *sokaiya* was provided. Seven were born overseas, including six foreign nationals (five from the United States and one from France) and one person born in Manchuria. Of the remaining *sokaiya*, 168 were born in Tokyo and thirty-three in Osaka. Surprisingly, another seventy-five (18.02 percent) were born in Hiroshima prefecture.

Hiroshima, Hyogo, and Fukuoka prefectures also rank

among the top five places of birth of *sokaiya*. These same areas are also regarded by the National Police Agency as hotbeds of organized criminal groups. The largest main-stream crime syndicate, Yamaguchi-gumi, is headquartered in Kobe in Hyogo prefecture.

Certainly part of the reason for the overrepresentation of certain geographic areas is the phenomenon of cliques (*kyodobatsu*) in Japan based on birthplace. These affilia-tions and common background can help facilitate a person's movement into a particular field. Also helping is the so-called *gakubatsu* or school clique. There is evidence of such cliques at work in the *sokaiya* population as well. Three *sokaiya* attended Takushoku University and two attended Kokushikan University. According to the dates of birth available, at least two of those attending Takushoku University likely knew each other in school. Other universities can claim their share of graduates turning to *sokaiya* work. These include eight who attended Meiji University, another eight from Waseda University, and one from Keio University. These three uni-versities are elite public schools with many of the graduates going into upper-level corporations on management tracks.

Group Structure

Sokaiya groups range in complexity from two- or three-man organizations to rather complex groupings. Small groups of a dozen or so individuals appear to be largely independent associations of *sokaiya* without any formal hierarchy but, instead, formal links to a particular leader. In turn, members may share other links with members of equal or lesser ranks.

However, many of the larger groups usually form them-selves into organizations that copy corporate hierarchies and bureaucracies. Individuals take on titles such as "chairman" (*kaicho*) or "director."

Rondan Doyu-kai, the largest group of *sokaiya*, is structured this way. At the top of the corporate group are a chairman and two chief directors who oversee separate five-man boards of directors. These groups set internal and external policies, publish a newspaper, and engage in other activities. The remaining members have no titles as such, but come under the direct leadership of the chairman and are linked to one or the other internal or external boards.

The average age of Rondan members was thirty-eight. There is evidence of birthplace and school cliques within the group as seventeen of the thirty-nine members were born in Hiroshima prefecture and eleven in Tokyo. The remainder come from scattered rural areas. Eleven of the members were graduates of universities or post-high-school-education facilities. Three of the members attended Senshu University. Since two of those members, Koichi Masada and Yoshiki Asada, were born in 1949 and the third, Masanori Asada, was born in 1946, it is likely they knew each other and had some contact with each other during their university days. It is not known if the two Asadas are related.

At the time of the group's description in the 1986 manual, all three held responsible positions within the group. Yoshiki Asada held the rank of *kanjicho* or management chief. Masanori Asada appeared in the ranks of the headquarters staff. Masada Koichi was listed in the group's branch staff.

The framework of the group as outlined in *Tanto-sha hikkei* offers a mix of the traditional conception of a hierarchical Japanese group and a more Western idea of a corporate organization.

At the top post is Masaki Tatsuki, *kaicho,* or chairman.

Directly beneath him are a *rijicho,* or chief director, and a *kanjicho,* or management chief. The *rijicho* presides over a seven-member *rijikai,* or directors' committee. This committee in turn oversees the sixteen-member branch section. Each director is linked with from one to four branch-section members. The lines of authority are quite distinct and apparently hierarchical. This is not the case in the eleven-member headquarters section under the guidance of a five-man management committee chaired by the *kanjicho.* Rondan's internal structure reflects a great deal of flexibility with the headquarters section. No man is directly linked to any other man but all appear to be answerable to the full management committee.

The rankings and titles the *sokaiya* give themselves are certainly important to them. Membership in a group, especially a large group with connections to mainstream organized-crime groups, is equally important. But all of these things are geared to one aim: the collection of money.

Payments to *Sokaiya*

One company manager who dealt with *sokaiya* reported that during the months prior to the annual shareholder meeting he would meet with dozens of *sokaiya* in a single day—sometimes as many as forty. His assistant would wear a special suit coat with pockets stitched into the lining. The pockets were marked "A" through "E," and each held sealed envelopes with a specific amount of cash inside. Never was there any discussion about payments. Indeed, the *sokaiya* knew his rank, and both manager and *sokaiya* knew what the proper payment would be. The source explained:

> It was important to keep them moving. We both understood why they came. If they had something important to say, we listened.

But otherwise it was a simple matter to signal the assistant to produce the proper envelope at the appropriate time and send the *sokaiya* on his way. We really don't want to get into a position where we have to spend a lot of time with them.... I always believe that when dealing with *sokaiya* you have to stay one level above them in terms of the attitude you take and language you use. You can never give them the advantage or they will take it. (Interview 1993)

One reason for this manager's system was that usually only the lower-ranking *sokaiya* would visit a company for a payoff.

Prior to the amendments to the Commercial Code, a large number of individuals who quite clearly had no ties with the commercial world could often be seen in the Marunouchi area (Tokyo's financial district), queuing outside the general affairs departments of their client companies. To prevent their attendance at meetings, or at least keep them silent on those occasions, companies would pay them off according to rank. It was generally recognized that only low-rank *sokaiya* queued outside companies because the high-rank *sokaiya* received their payments at *ryotei* (high-class Japanese restaurants). (Isaacs and Ejiri 1990, 125)

Visits by *sokaiya* would often net them a respectable amount of pocket money, ranging from one thousand to two thousand yen for an "E"-class *sokaiya*, two thousand to three thousand yen for a "D"-class, and up to ten thousand or more (usually more) for an "A"-class. Among *sokaiya*, the expected amount of payment may be larger or smaller depending upon the industrial sector of the paying company—large from banks, small from less wealthy firms. The payments themselves have nicknames, as explained by one long-time observer of *sokaiya*:

> From banks, [payments are called] monthly income; from se-
> curities companies, year-end bonuses; from regular companies,
> regular spending money. Further, using organizations such as
> "economic research centers" or "economic investigation groups"
> [as covers], they hand over receipts with their *meishi* [business
> cards] attached and companies hand back money. ("Zoka suru
> Boryoku-sokaiya no gokuhi o hatsukokai" 1978, 84)

A *sokaiya* could expect additional payments if he provided a
particularly valuable service. However, a high-ranking *sokaiya*
would seldom demand a specific amount for his services; rather,
he would rely on the company manager to determine the appropriate payment. In the late 1970s, when the *sokaiya* population
was at its peak (some five to six thousand persons), estimates
placed the average yearly income for "A"-class *sokaiya* at between 200 and 300 million yen, 40 to 50 million yen for "B"-
class, 5 to 6 million yen for "C"-class, 3 to 4 million yen for
"D"-class, and between 1 and 2 million for "E"-class ("Sokaiya
no mitsuida kigyo 240–sha risuto" 1978b, 121).

Although at present there are no clear estimates on monthly
payments to *sokaiya* by corporations, in the past such information was collected and published by the Japanese National Police Agency (NPA). For example, in 1978 and 1980
the NPA reported the results of their surveys of corporations
that had held shareholder meetings in June of those years
and were listed on the Tokyo Stock Exchange.

In 1978, the NPA surveyed 455 companies about their
payments to *sokaiya*. Seventy-three companies (20.1 percent) reported that the cost of dealing with *sokaiya* was about
one million yen or less per year. Three firms reported expenses topping 100 million per year. Further, 156 firms (44.3
percent) said they paid each *sokaiya* between 10,000 and
100,000 yen. Seventy firms (19.9 percent) said they paid

between 110,000 and 200,000 yen per *sokaiya*. One company reported paying more than one billion yen to a single *sokaiya* ("Keishicho, sokaiya ni kan suru chosa kekka wo happyo" 1978, 36).

In 1980, 440 companies were surveyed by the police. Seventy-six companies (22.1 percent) reported paying about one million yen to all *sokaiya*. Five firms acknowledged paying at least 100 million yen. Another company reported paying 350 million yen, and two firms said they made total payments of between 351 million and one billion yen.

At 115 companies (34.4 percent), payments per *sokaiya* ranged from 10,000 to 20,000 yen. Eighty-three companies (24.6 percent) made payments ranging from 5,001 to 10,000 yen. Fifty-two companies (15.5 percent) paid between 20,000 and 30,000 yen. Two companies (0.6 percent) reported paying 100,000 yen per *sokaiya*, and three firms (0.9 percent) reportedly paid more than 100,000 yen per *sokaiya* ("Keishicho, sokaiya nado ni kan suru chosa kekku matomeru" 1980, 40).

Local police, too, surveyed companies within their jurisdictions. For example, in 1979, the police in Kanagawa prefecture (bordering Tokyo and including the port of Yokohama) surveyed fifty firms. According to their survey, twenty-five companies made one-time special payments to *sokaiya* ranging from 50,000 yen to 120,000 yen (average payment 70,000 yen). The lowest payments ranged from 1,000 yen to 30,000 yen (average payment 6,000 yen). One company paid from 50,000 to as much as 9 million yen in one-time special payments.

The firms reported to the police that they made the payments, not for help at meetings, but as tokens of goodwill during such occasions as the opening of new offices by *sokaiya* groups, gifts for the anniversaries of the establishment of *sokaiya* groups, special entertainment fees, and fees for seminars, research meetings, and golf competitions produced by *sokaiya*. Twenty-six of the companies reportedly used a "manager *sokaiya*" at all times, while twenty-four companies denied such a practice ("Kanagawa-Kenkatsu, sokaiya nado ni kan suru jittai chosa matomeru" 1979, 40–41).

These "manager *sokaiya*," usually holding the "A" rank, provide ongoing consultation and protection to companies—a sort of hired security service. In return, they could expect a huge income from payoffs. One *sokaiya*, for example, arrested in 1977, received approximately 300 million yen from 771 companies in the form of support payments (*sanjokin*), magazine subscriptions, and other benefits. In the first six months of 1977 he was paid 31 million yen by twenty financial institutions alone, with 5 million coming from a single bank (Nakabayashi 1978, 655–56). In another incident during 1977, police found one *sokaiya* who held 110 million yen in cash in various bank-branch deposit boxes of two city banks (Japan's major national banks). In May of that year, the police and National Tax Agency calculated that this particular *sokaiya*'s income from 1974 to 1977 was some 209 million yen. He was forced to pay 88 million yen in back taxes. In yet another arrest, a major *sokaiya* in the Kansai region earned 16.9 million yen from 170 companies in 1974, 33.4 million yen from 185 companies in 1975, 28.3 million yen from 171 companies in 1976, and 45.1 million yen from 184 companies between January and October 1977, netting him an estimated four-year gross income of 123.8 million yen ("Sokaiya no mitsuida kigyo 240–sha risuto" 1978, 122).

One survey conducted by the Osaka branch of the National Tax Agency revealed that the five largest banks in Osaka in the mid-1970s—Sanwa, Daiwa, Sumitomo, Taiyo-Kobe, and Sumitomo Trust—paid *sokaiya* some 500 million yen from October 1975 through September 1976. An additional ten regional banks in Osaka and Kyoto paid a total of 300 million yen to *sokaiya*. All of the money was listed on the agency's survey as "*sokaiya* countermeasure Fees" *(sokaiya taisaku-hi)*. Following the 1982 Commercial Code reform, this category would necessarily disappear, as payments to *sokaiya* became illegal. But they did not become impossible to make and the law could be easily circumvented. Companies are still able to partially write off such fees by including them in such deductible categories as magazine subscriptions, reading materials, and advertising fees. One city bank paid 300 million yen in these fees in a single year, while another bank allotted 500,000 yen monthly for payment to a single *sokaiya*, adding an additional one million yen for participation in a golf competition arranged by the *sokaiya* and yet another million yen for a party celebrating the founding of his organization.

Still, not all fees are accounted for by operating expenses, but instead they are often listed as "unaccounted expenditures" *(shito fumeikin)*. Some fifteen banks in the region spent an additional one billion yen on such unaccounted expenditures, and although they were forced to pay a 50-million-yen tax on this spending, they declined to explain the payments further. Thus, one expert on *sokaiya* wrote:

> The financial sources of *sokaiya* are only partially revealed by such surveys for two reasons. First, banks want to maintain an outward appearance of trustworthiness and are reluctant to explain unaccounted expenditures. Second, banks do not want to explain their connections to *sokaiya* but prefer to protect the information about their connections and thus protect the *sokaiya*. (Kawamoto 1979b, 91)

Although no detailed accounting of recent *sokaiya*-income estimates is available, it is possible to assess the magnitude of the money still circulating between corporations and *sokaiya* when *sokaiya* and corporate executives are arrested by police. Between 1982 and 1992, there were twenty-two arrests for violations of Commercial Code Article 497 (discussed later in detail) which prohibits the use of corporate funds to purchase the exercise of shareholder rights. In a single incident in 1992, illegal payoffs to *sokaiya* totaled 27 million yen—the largest amount since code reform until a year later, when Kirin Beer executives and eight *sokaiya* were arrested. The total payoff to those *sokaiya* is said to have been 33 million yen. But police believe Kirin's payments to these *sokaiya* over several years probably topped 100 million yen (Kasahara 1993; "Sokaiya to no yuchaku wo kotonare" 1993, 2).

Although the payoffs have been huge and remain so, they are merely indications of the depth to which corrupt officials and organized criminal groups collaborate in the purchasing and delivery of services. More than the payments, the complexity of the organization, the nicknames, the rankings, and the organizational structure (including the mimicking of corporate executive titles within *sokaiya* organizations) demonstrate how intricate are the ties between the corporations of Japan and that nation's underworld. But another element needs to be explored—the *sokaiya*'s self-perpetuation within the corporate system. Their history, while not as long or even bloody as the *yakuza*'s, reveals in even greater depth how each institution (the corporate and the criminal) protects the other.

Notes

1. There were numerous journalistic accounts of the Suzuki killing for several days following his death. For example, see Ihara and Hamada 1994, 69, and *Shukan toyo keizai* 1994, 38, for more analytical treat-

ments of the Suzuki murder. Articles in other major Japanese newspapers providing police accounts of the slaying ran largely from March 1 through March 3, 1994.

2. The data contained in the annual white paper of shareholder meetings published by *Shoji homu* are analyzed in a separate chapter.

3. The book containing Taniguchi's writing was provided by an individual who has studied *sokaiya* as part of his work for a Japanese corporation. The book was privately published in the 1970s by Keiichi Ariyama, a known *sokaiya*. Ariyama was attempting to distance himself from the field by publishing materials which might be of help to companies investigating contacts received from *sokaiya*.

2

Sokaiya Foundations
and History

Most shareholder meetings in Japan are held annually on the last Thursday in June. The few weeks before that day are so busy with sokaiya *activities, they are popularly called the "*sokaiya *season" by the public and media.*

On the day of a meeting, it is not unusual to see hordes of men bustling out of company buildings. Some are clearly shareholders who, alone, hurry along the streets or await their limousines. They carry small shopping bags containing a few trinkets distributed by the company to attendees. Others, traveling in boisterous groups, are obviously sokaiya. *Conversations are alternately angry and merry. Follow them, and they talk of inept questions, failed strategies, big victories. It is a typical scene in the business district on shareholder-meeting day.*

On one occasion, however, the relative normalcy was disrupted. Blaring pseudomilitary music sounded, echoing off the tall buildings. Around a corner came a huge black reconverted bus, its windows covered with thick screens, its sides draped with banners, its top studded with huge speakers and rising-sun battle flags. The right wing had arrived.

The bus stopped in front of the building housing the corporate headquarters of a ball-bearing company recently rocked by an insider-trading scandal. A man, clad in a black jumpsuit, emerged from the bus. Climbing

34

atop the bus, holding a microphone, he made a passionate speech about corporate corruption and how it, along with political corruption, is weakening Japan—which in his view should be dominating the world. The speech finished, the uniformed man descended and entered the bus. The music blared again. The bus drove away. The scene returned to its normal bustle.

While not an everyday event, the above scene is hardly rare, and such has been the case in Japan for one hundred years. Simply put, if businessmen did not want or need *sokaiya*, *sokaiya* would not exist. *Sokaiya*, in other words, are the corporate world's "necessary evil" or *hitsuyo aku*. How did this happen? Where did the *sokaiya* come from? Why have they not been eradicated? Japanese organized-crime syndicates have a long history, shrouded in myth. There is no mystery about *sokaiya*, however. They exist because they offer services businessmen want. They remain because they know how to manipulate those wants to their advantage and are thus self-perpetuating. So in this chapter I will trace the history of *sokaiya* into the modern era.

Early Days

When *sokaiya* first emerged in the late nineteenth century, no modern commercial law governing business operations in Japan existed. Consequently, the country's burgeoning economic modernization was plagued by a wide variety of abuses. Legal reformers in and out of government constantly raised these abuses as reasons to establish a basic company law. Fraud and bankruptcies were common facets of early joint-stock-corporation formation. Since there was no official legal concept of limited liability, investors risked their entire fortunes, not merely their investment, on a business that could collapse overnight (Fukushima 1991, 173–81).

"Pawnbrokers, second-hand furniture dealers and money

changers" dominated the securities markets. The stock exchange itself resembled

> a gambling den [more] than a serious capital market. Companies issued shares to be paid for by installments, while investors borrowed bank money to purchase the shares, pledging [the shares] to the banks as security. The vast majority of transactions were in futures, and a huge proportion of them involved the shares of the [Tokyo] Stock Exchange itself. (Clark 1979, 34)

As a result, just underneath the system of expanding capitalism, there existed a second system, populated by individuals involved in all manner of risky ventures, fraud, insider trading, price-fixing, market cornering, and so on. Rumor, innuendo, speculation, good information, and outright lies fueled this market manipulation. Information, no matter how obviously untrue, could destroy a company and its investors. Thus when an individual invested in a company, that person was literally gambling on its reputation. Not surprisingly, those with the wit and ability to turn such situations to their advantage were drawn to this environment. Among them were the so-called founders of the *sokaiya* profession, Inokichi Chiharu and Kosaku Takebe. Both men are credited with establishing the basic patterns of actions used for and against companies even today.[1]

Inokichi Chiharu

Chiharu gained fame from the end of the Meiji Era (1868–1911) through the Taisho Era (1912–25) by stock speculation and by offering his services as a *sokaiya*. Typically, he would bring a large number of his followers to meetings, and they would praise management if paid and criticize management if not paid or if his group was employed by others to act against the managers.

Chiharu's intention was to intervene so that he could gain

greater access to management and information about corpora-tions, which in turn would further aid him in stock speculation and *sokaiya* work. His career was shaken in 1913, however, af-ter one of his underlings published an exposé in Chiharu's maga-zine, *Tokyo jiji tsushin* (Tokyo Current News Circular). As a result, Chiharu was arrested for blackmail. He hired defense at-torney Takuzo Hanai (1868–1931), a native of Hiroshima prefec-ture who had studied at Tokyo's English Law School, the predecessor of Chuo University, as well as attending Tokyo Law School. Hanai was famous for handling criminal defense cases and eventually became a professor at Chuo University, president of the Tokyo Bar Association, and a member for several terms in the House of Representatives, where he served as speaker (Kamesaka 1926, 6; Rengo Press 1965, 231).

In the end, Chiharu was acquitted, and Hanai became a lead-ing talent scout for Chiharu, sending him young men who might serve as new trainees. Hanai was particularly interested in men who were familiar with the Commercial Code and who could engage in strong, legally based debates, as such skills were im-portant in raising the status of *sokaiya* beyond that of mere thugs. If a *sokaiya* could display even a facile knowledge of company law and demonstrate it on his feet in a shareholder meeting against the shouts and threats of opposing *sokaiya*, he could become a valuable resource for management or others willing to pay for such skills. One such man recruited by Hanai was Yuzaburo Kubo, who would dominate the *sokaiya* world before World War II and for several decades after (Minato 1979, 44–46).

Kosaku Takebe

Kosaku Takebe, Chiharu's contemporary, began his career not as a *sokaiya* but as a lobbyist for the Liberal Party (*Jiyu-to*). He changed careers in the early twentieth century when he assumed control of a five-thousand-man gambling syndicate following the death of its leader, Kichigoro Inoue. These gambling groups, known within the *yakuza* as *bakuto*, were one of the two main types of *yakuza* operating in Japan at the time. The other, *tekiya*, ran entertainment operations at large and small festivals around the nation.

Takebe used the profits gained from gambling to buy his way into the business world. He soon became linked with a leading businessman, Seinosuke Go, who used Takebe's underworld connections to provide protective services for major corporations, particularly utility companies.

Go (1865–1942), a native of Gifu prefecture, graduated from Doshisha College and Tokyo University and received his Ph.D. in Europe. He became an official at the Department of Agriculture and Commerce and president of Nippon Transportation Company, as well as a director of both the Nippon Fire Insurance Company and Oji Paper Manufacturing Company, and president of the Tokyo Paper Manufacturing Company. As board chairman of Tokyo Electric Light Company, he guided the firm from near bankruptcy to being the nation's most financially powerful utility. He was a member of the House of Peers, president of the Japan Chamber of Commerce and Industry, president of the Tokyo Stock Exchange, and adviser to the Bank of Japan (Kamesaka 1926, 28; Rengo Press 1965, 208).

Especially for a gambler such as Takebe, the lure of quick profits made by placing a bet (buying stock) in a particular company would be enticing. Moreover, if scandal about the company could be dredged up, resulting in its share price plummeting, one could make a fortune if one's futures contract had that particular stock closing at a lower price. In other words, stock speculation helped drive the *sokaiya* field as companies hired their own *sokaiya* to protect the company name, attack competitors, and serve as intelligence operatives. But far more importantly, the interaction between *sokaiya* such as Chiharu and Takebe and powerful legal and commercial leaders like lawyer Hanai and businessman Go placed *sokaiya* at the nexus of the business world. It is clear that, rather than distance, business leaders sought out and courted the friendship of underworld figures.

Early Patterns

Usually *sokaiya* acted quietly and behind the scenes, as in the case of Ryutaro Fukao, one of their many victims. He, like Go, was a member of the House of Peers and president of Nisshin Kissen, a steamship company headquartered in Osaka. He graduated from Tokyo Higher Commercial College, worked briefly for Osaka Shosen Kaisha (another shipping company), and served in the armed forces during the Russo-Japanese War. His chief career interest was steamship lines, leading him to become first a manager of the Tokyo and Yokohama branches of the Osaka Shosen Company and later a director of Kaigai Kogyo Corporation, Chosen Yusen Company, and the South America Development Company, all shipping and transportation companies.

Fukao became the victim of *sokaiya* pressure at a regular shareholder meeting prior to World War II. It is not clear from the available report exactly when the incident took place or what the dispute involved, and the details of the meeting are sketchy, but the following example reveals how *sokaiya* were able to demonstrate their ability to manipulate a meeting with mere silence.

Approximately thirty shareholders were in attendance at the meeting in Osaka. Fukao attempted to pass a set of bills after making a speech supporting them. His request for a voice vote from the shareholders was met with silence. Using extremely polite language, Fukao asked the shareholders if there was a problem with the bills. Still he received no response.

Fukao finally managed to cajole the crowd into voting, thus ending the meeting. He then met with his employees, accusing them of being nothing more than "scarecrows" since they had stood quietly by as he wrestled alone with the imposing silence. Finally, one employee explained that the shareholders had been too frightened to vote, as a *sokaiya* had threatened them just before the meeting. Fukao, who had refused to make payoffs to *sokaiya* in the past, later hired Yuzaburo Kubo (mentioned above), an underling of Chiharu, to handle all future meetings. Fukao's instructions to Kubo were simple: no matter what happened in the meeting, Kubo was to give full support of management's bills and take whatever steps necessary to end the meeting without incident. It is entirely possible that Kubo himself was the *sokaiya* who had conducted the silent intimidation campaign, showing Fukao in concrete terms why he (Kubo) should be employed.

The use of *sokaiya* was not limited to those companies trading shares on the open market. *Zaibatsu* families, who owned vast industrial and financial empires dominated by a holding company that handled all major policy decisions, made heavy use of *sokaiya* in their intrafamily struggles. Although the holding company might be managed by a particularly skilled individual, called a *banto* (manager), actual decisions were made, based on the *banto*'s advice, by the family whose members were major stockholders. As in all families, conflicts occasionally arose, but rather than fight among themselves, the family employed *sokaiya* who fought out policy and succession battles at shareholder meetings (Okumura 1986, 70).

Although there is little documentary evidence about *sokaiya* development in the first half of the twentieth century, some thumbnail sketches of *sokaiya* do exist. Most concern *sokaiya* who established their careers prior to World War II and who were able to continue under new conditions following Allied Occupation changes to the Commercial Code. Several sketches, along with a post–World War II *sokaiya* history, were collected into a thin volume by Toyoharu Kanda, himself a *sokaiya*, who allegedly quit the profession in the 1980s (Kanda 1991). The sketches suggest the types of individuals who entered the early *sokaiya* field. The following are examples gleaned from Kanda's work.

Masamitsu Tajima attended Meiji University but quit school after becoming linked with a number of right-wing organizations and joining in the colonization of Manchuria. In 1932 he was involved in a dispute among shareholders of a large bus company. The company's founder hired Tajima to fend off assaults by the Takebe *sokaiya* group. He was so effective that Takebe threatened to kill him. In order to avoid death, Tajima met with a Takebe underling at Takebe's home. There, he joined in a *sakezuke*, a ritual in which cups of sake are passed between men who then, after drinking from the cups, become fictive brothers. Eventually Tajima became second in command of the Takebe organization.

Shoichi Taniguchi was born in Yamaguchi prefecture. He attended Ritsumeikan University and was drafted into the army and stationed in China during World War I. He became known among *sokaiya* and corporate managers for his extremely skilled window-dressing settlements (in which a company's accounts are made to appear better than they actually are) and his highly developed ability to read and analyze accounting data which he could turn against corporations. He recruited other Ritsumeikan graduates, including Eiji Shimazaki, a major figure in postwar conflicts between social-protest groups and large corporations that employed *sokaiya* as mercenary forces.

These profiles and the earlier brief sketches of Chiharu and Takebe suggest some important fundamental aspects of *sokaiya*. The *sakezuke* ritual and Takebe's involvement in a gambling organization point to ties to *yakuza* from the start. The *sakezuke* is particularly important as a method for settling disputes or linking groups among gangsters. Moreover, in modern times, photographs are taken showing who is in attendance at such events. The extent of the support for individuals on both sides can be clearly displayed, and one's position in the group portrait indicates closeness of affiliation (the closer to the central figures, the closer to the center of power).

Just as important, many of these men were highly educated and able to move around easily in the business world. Chiharu was a newspaper publisher—no mean feat, even if the publication is run for extortion purposes, as is the case with many *sokaiya* today. Takebe had, in addition to his skills as a gambler, the necessary social skills, as well as street savvy, to act as a lobbyist for a major political group. Both Tajima and Taniguchi attended prestigious universities, and a fair number of *sokaiya*, even today, have had university educations or have graduated from special technical schools (*senmon gakko*), where they receive a basic education in fields important to *sokaiya* operations—law, economics, finance, and even computer databases and data processing. These men then are able to hone their skills after entering *sokaiya* groups, much like their fellow Japanese-university graduates who receive several years of additional training once they enter a corporation.

Informal Private Security

Clearly, one can begin to understand why *sokaiya* are often deemed a "necessary evil" among Japanese corporate managers. In the largely unregulated period of corporate growth prior to 1893, personal fortunes were extremely vulnerable to the manipulation of information that could damage the company's status, the investors' stakes, or both. Following legal reform in the late nineteenth century, even though personal fortunes were no longer at high risk through the imposition of limited-liability regulations, investors could be persuaded to remove their funding from a corporation on the basis of unsavory rumors. A hint of doubt, coupled with the centuries-old views of business as unclean and businessmen as less than honorable, could send investors fleeing. By the same token, rumors of potential success could draw investors to otherwise unstable ventures. Given these conditions, the early entrepreneurs of Japan would find it only reasonable to hire protection. In this they would not be different from other groups around the world who employ people to provide protection on an informal basis when formal, government-sanctioned protection is unavailable or inadequate.

Formal private-security forces, regulated by the state, are an extremely recent phenomenon in Japan, first established in 1962 to bolster police forces assigned to protect the 1964 Olympic Games facilities (Miyazawa 1991). Prior to that, those seeking protection beyond any provided by the police had to do so on an informal basis. The early *sokaiya* were available for the protection of businessmen, particularly in instances where their own or their company's reputation or business activities would be publicly threatened. Whether in Japan or elsewhere, the fact that such individuals could act against an individual or corporation while protecting others of similar status is one of the main characteristics of these groups.

Like the Mafia in Italy, these informal security groups survive over time at least partly because of the nature of the services they provide:

> The continuity of the Mafia, if only in its capacity for profound transformation, derives from the fact that the Mafia's behavior has always been a specific combination of ancient and modern, a mixture of private violence and the legitimate violence of the state, of competition for economic resources in the market and the absence of regulatory standards for economic activities other than violence. (Catanzaro 1985, 35)

Japan's elites, like those in other societies, have long recruited their informal private-security forces from underworld or fringe groups. Moreover, there is a tradition of corruption through co-operation with formal state forces. For example, after the criminal-police system was reorganized in 1805, the marshals in charge of the central office in the area around Tokyo made a pact with bandit groups: in return for keeping their own activities in check, the police would conduct raids against rival groups (DeVos and Mizushima 1967, 296).

Another example of informal security in Japan is the so-called *shoshi*, which is literally translated as "heroic knight," but is often used as a synonym for "political hireling" or "thug." *Shoshi* came from the ranks of ex-samurai who were no longer guaranteed their yearly stipend of rice under the reforms of the Meiji government. The ultranationalist group, the Dark Ocean Society, was comprised chiefly of *shoshi* who carried out violent acts against opposing political leaders. Late twentieth century violent groups (*boryokudan* in police parlance), such as gangsters (*yakuza*) in organized-crime syndicates, ultranationalists (*uyokuha*), and *sokaiya*, are more modern equivalents.

Sokaiya gained a foothold in the Japanese corporate system largely due to the inadequacies of the formal legal system. The concept of the corporation was relatively unknown in Japan and did not have the generations of development and cultural underpinnings that it did in European nations. Consequently, the concept of the rights and responsibilities of the investor was also undeveloped. Information about corporations and those running them was an important resource for investors, since that information could be manipulated in a variety of ways to drive a share price up or down. Individual investors could place "bets" on the future performance of a corporation using "wagers" in the form of bank loans collateralized by the very shares bought with the loan money. Thus, protecting the reputation of the corporation and its managers and manipulating information about them were of vital importance.

In sum, *sokaiya* early on offered useful tools for information and public-image manipulation. They were intelligent men, some even possessing valuable university educations in important fields. They recognized the usefulness and power of the printed word, and those who developed expertise in accounting could assist a troubled corporation in arranging its books to avoid scandal. Since they were insiders of the *sokaiya*-corporate system, they could predict strategies that opponents of management might use against various measures at shareholder meetings. Moreover, since some were willing to employ violence or the threat of violence to intimidate others, they were able to offer services that regular white-collar employees or advisers could not. All of these resources could be turned against a corporation manager or owner who would otherwise prefer not to deal with *sokaiya* at all.

But perhaps the most important attribute possessed by the successful *sokaiya* is adaptability. The changes wrought on Japan by the Allied Occupation created new rules, changed old ones, and provided an array of new resources that *sokaiya* could draw upon.

Corporate Ownership and Control

At the end of World War II, the Allied powers, dominated by the United States, targeted the holding companies of *zaibatsu* (large-scale industrial groups) for reform or dissolution. Reform recommendations were based on the findings of the 1946 U.S. Department of State Mission on Japanese Combines, led by Corwin D. Edwards. The findings were an indictment of prewar Japanese corporate operations. Of particular interest are the comments the mission gathered on the role of the shareholder, ostensibly the owner of the corporation. In the Japanese corporate system

> the relationship between stockholders and management in the *zaibatsu*-controlled corporations is a distillation of the most objectionable features to be found in other economies. To begin with, the stockholders of any corporation are divided into two groups—those who control, and others. In practice the identity of the two groups is never in question. Both groups look upon the corporation as being the property of the *zaibatsu* stockholders. (*RMJC* 1946, 22)

The commission expected to find what it viewed as the basic checks and balances that help govern a corporation and provide basic norms of corporate ownership and control—but they were missing. The commission reported that

> in a Japanese *zaibatsu* company, a proxy fight is not simply unusual; it borders on the inconceivable. Stockholder suits to recover damages, to compel payment of dividends, or to remove management in such corporations are scarcely within the scope of Japanese conception. (Ibid.)

In blunter terms, the commission included this note to the general discussion: "The universal reaction of Japanese businessmen to questions on the status of the stockholder was to explain that in Japan 'the stockholder has nothing to say'" (ibid.).

Stockholders "had nothing to say" because there was no need for management to listen to them. Individual investors outside the controlling family were not a major source of capital in the case of larger corporations, which had learned to insulate themselves from market swings. Instead, banks from the same corporate group provided normal sources of financing. Corporations could arrange sufficient financing either through loans or cross-shareholdings with other corporations, a holding company, or the group's bank. Companies avoided paying high dividends to attract investors because major shareholders were not interested in either dividends or capital gains; instead, they held shares for security. Moreover, management seldom had to concern itself with paying back the money the corporation borrowed, since the group lenders normally were concerned only that the company pay back interest on the debt.

Such behavior, in place for just five decades before World War II, short-circuited public involvement in the corporate system. Although the Allied investigating commission viewed these practices as the worst forms of capitalist development, they were the intended outcome of Yataro Iwasaki, founder of the Mitsubishi *zaibatsu* and the progenitor of Japan's banking system. Iwasaki deliberately steered Japan on a course modeled on the European continental universal bank. Under that system, bank loans supported a new company until it could raise sufficient capital in the public securities market. Once the corporation proved able to stand on its own, the bank sold a portion of its holdings to trustworthy and reliable investors who had high standing with the bank. The bank "would continue to have a controlling voice, since the private investors, with whom the bank had placed the shares of the enterprise, would continue to hold their shares in the custody of the bank and vote their shares through the bank" (Drucker 1975, 231).

The practice united the investors into an extended "family" of trusted individuals.

> This characteristic Japanese phenomenon of family enterprises linked together in the same combine chain of capital, headed by a top holding company, carried over certain unprogressive aspects derived from feudal times. Its main evil was its basic premise which discouraged maximum participation by the Japanese public at large in widespread ownership of the larger enterprises, relegating it to the unenviable position of those undeserving of any vitally significant role in economic affairs. (Salwin 1962, 489)

Iwasaki argued that the general public should never be allowed to interfere in the running of any corporation, since the corporation was intrinsic to the strength of the state. Thus the government, one of the major shareholders within the prewar corporate system in Japan, saw little practical benefit in enforcing shareholder rights or including the general public in the corporate decision-making process. The rationale was that it was unthinkable to spread corporate ownership in the hands of the public, who could not be relied upon to see any greater view beyond its own pocketbook. Only troublemakers, it was believed, would raise questions about a corporation's management, since the company's main bank and the bank's group of trusted investors maintained tight control of major blocks of a company's shares.

This belief is still prevalent today, as is the long-standing view that only troublemakers or *sokaiya* raise questions. In the words of one source, who claimed it was easy to spot *sokaiya*: "They are the only ones who ask questions [at shareholder meetings]. Anyone who asks a question is a *sokaiya*." Although an exaggeration, his point is that speaking out in a shareholder meeting is a signal that the individual is an outsider—which is as true today as it was in the few years after World War II, when

Allied reforms to correct this situation were set in motion. If one is an insider, one does not need to ask questions.

Occupation Reforms

The reforms brought about by the Occupation government are themselves well known, but a short review is necessary. (See Bisson 1954; Yamamura 1967; and Hadley 1970, among others, for more comprehensive discussions.)

The Supreme Commander of the Allied Powers (SCAP) declared its intent to liquidate and reapportion *zaibatsu* capital, whether that capital was found in holding companies, their subsidiaries, or major affiliated banks. The allies saw the roots of the war as embedded in the fertile ground of capitalist expansion led by the *zaibatsu*. These corporate groups cooperated with the Japanese government in the overseas expansion of the Japanese empire to secure steady supplies of natural resources in order to further industrial growth. SCAP targeted *zaibatsu* companies for a total breakup, divesting *zaibatsu* families and executives from majority stock ownership, and breaking the capital interlocks between affiliates, subsidiaries, and the major credit banks (Edwards 1946).

> The reform was to be thoroughgoing . . . the economic structure visualized . . . was totally alien. Throughout her industrial history, Japan had never had a competitive economic system. Formerly, the government had fostered the power of *zaibatsu* monopolies, helped to organize and to enforce cartels and encouraged mergers of larger market-leading firms. It was not the Japanese way to enforce competition, to disallow all types of cartels, or to encourage a wide dispersion of stockholding. (Yamamura 1967, 3)

As Bisson points out, such concepts were not only unknown in the system but were unwelcome:

> A free enterprise economy had no roots in Japanese development. The urge for land on the part of the peasantry supplied a strong natural force to back the [SCAP] land reform program. There was no comparable force operating in favor of competitive enterprise in business. Few independent business enterprises of size or importance had survived the war. Free enterprise could be labeled un-Japanese in the sense that socialism is sometimes called un-American. Japan knew the *zaibatsu* combines, the hybrid national policy companies, and state-operated enterprises like the railways. A competitive economy, regulated by government to maintain competition, Japan did not know. No favoring climate of opinion existed; the Occupation would have to create it. (Bisson 1954, 40-41)

Share-Ownership Redistribution

A large portion of this creative task went to the Holding Company Liquidation Committee (HCLC), formed on November 6, 1945. HCLC members, all Japanese, identified eighty-three firms as holding companies belonging to ten *zaibatsu* groups. The committee acted quickly, dissolving forty-two companies by the end of 1947; the rest were reorganized. The dissolution included the liquidation and redistribution of shares to the public. HCLC received 165.6 million shares plus bonds and other corporate securities valued at 7.75 billion yen. An additional 500 million yen in shares was taken directly from *zaibatsu* family members.

As a result of the redistribution of shares to the public, by 1949, individuals held some 69.1 percent of all securities. The remainder was distributed between the national and local governments (2.8 percent), financial institutions (9.9 percent), securities companies (12.6 percent), and corporations (5.6 percent). Since 1949, however, there has been a gradual erosion of individual-share ownership, with corporations and financial institutions soaking up the shares (Repeta 1988, 114). Nearly fifty years later, Japanese financial institutions, especially insurance companies, hold 45 percent of outstanding shares of Japanese corporations. Japanese corporations themselves hold nearly 25 percent, while individuals hold about 20.2 percent (Kawamoto et al. 1993, 17).

Strengthened Shareholder Rights

In addition to SCAP redistribution of corporate securities, shareholder rights were strengthened in a major reform of the Commercial Code in 1950. The reform was modeled after changes in the U.S. commercial legal system enacted after the 1929 stock-market crash, including the Securities Act of 1933 and the Securities Exchange Act of 1934, both of which led to the formation of the U.S. Securities and Exchange Commission. The laws and the commission were intended to protect U.S. consumers through disclosure of information at the time of sale of securities. Other reforms imposed on the Japanese were intended to provide shareholders with access to basic information about how a company they invested in was being run.

> As a general rule, corporate management [in Japan] was considered neither responsive nor responsible to the shareholders . . . . Code provisions embraced a system of protected corporate management antithetical to the shareholders in general and to minority shareholders in particular. The underlying theory was that the original promoters . . . and management group represented a set of interests distinct from that of the shareholders. . . . The

ordinary shareholder had no right of access to corporate books and records for the purpose of intelligently informing himself of suspected mismanagement. (Salwin 1962, 480)

Thus the changes in Japan's Commercial Code just after the war were intended to adjust the prewar attitudes and values among Japanese managers, owners, and elite third parties. Legal reform was targeted at resolving a variety of conflicts and dilemmas that reformers believed aided and abetted the formation of Japan's military-industrial complex. The redistribution of shares and the strengthened shareholder rights of disclosure were intended to shift power into the hands of the public.

Ownership and Control Disputes

Following the Occupation, the Japanese corporate system began to experience the first rumblings of what would become major challenges to the ownership and control of the nation's companies. Initially these challenges were low-intensity disputes involving a few individuals using the Allied reforms for their own benefit. However, the same reforms eventually provided resources to groups of pollution protesters and peace activists who used them to engage in widespread challenges to entire industries and industrial groupings. *Sokaiya* were the one consistent feature in all these conflicts, acting as intermediaries, advocates for other shareholders or themselves, or as management's informal private-security forces.

The Shirokiya Case

One of the most famous early postwar disputes began in 1952 and involved the notorious takeover artist, Hideki Yokoi. Yokoi was heavily involved in black-market operations, thanks to his position as a purveyor for the American Occupation forces, and this put him in touch with organized-crime groups, industrialists, and major power brokers, as well as providing him with a steady and large flow of cash. He would later become involved in one of Japan's great postwar scandals when his Hotel New Japan in Tokyo was destroyed by fire and thirty-three persons lost their lives due to an inadequate sprinkler system.

Yokoi began purchasing blocks of shares of the Shirokiya department store in 1952. In March 1954 he announced that he held more than 40 percent of the firm's outstanding shares. He demanded at a shareholder meeting that he be named a representative director (*daihyo torishimariyaku*) since, according to his calculations, he held even more shares than the firm's president. This was hotly disputed by the president, but, using the new Commercial Code provisions provided by the Allied reforms, Yokoi inspected the firm's books and found that 770,000 shares the president claimed to own actually belonged to the corporation—a violation of Commercial Code Article 210, which prohibited a company from acquiring its own shares except in special circumstances (EHS 1991, 52). The violation could become embarrassing for the company if a major conflict developed.

At the shareholder meeting, the argument between Yokoi—with *sokaiya* support—and management raged for two hours. Eventually the disputants reached a temporary compromise: a ten-member steering committee (*gijitsuko iin*) would be established to settle the matter. Each side chose three representatives who would argue their case before four intermediaries. Among the members of the steering committee were highly respected *sokaiya*, including Yuzaburo Kubo, who had been introduced to *sokaiya* progenitor Inokichi Chiharu by his attorney, Takuzo Hanai, decades before.

The committee failed to reach a settlement after more than a year of wrangling, and the dispute went to the Tokyo District Court. In July 1955 the court found that the company had illegally acquired its own shares and ordered them sold. They were bought by the Tokyu group, a major department-store and railway company owned by Keita Goto, a close associate of Yokoi. Today, Shirokiya is part of the Tokyu Nihonbashi store of Tokyu's chain of department stores and occupies a premier location in central Tokyo near the fashionable Ginza shopping district.

It remains unclear what Yokoi's intentions were regarding the shares, but several motives seem plausible. He may actually have hoped to gain a seat on Shirokiya's board. Perhaps he had hoped to obtain a greenmail payoff from the company in which he would sell back his shares at a premium in return for dropping his claim. Or he may have staged the dispute as part of a larger takeover attempt by Goto, who had Yokoi run interference for him. The details and actual reasons for the dispute are less important for this discussion than the fact that *sokaiya* were among those entrusted with the fate of a corporation's ownership, control, and reputation.

Sokaiya figures represented both sides in what must have been a difficult and highly technical series of negotiations. Where U.S. corporations will employ lawyers to attempt settlement of disputes, the Japanese will call upon individuals who may not be lawyers in Japan but are nonetheless knowledgeable about commercial law. In the Shirokiya dispute, *sokaiya*, being deeply familiar with all aspects of the Japanese Commercial Code as well as the interests of the two parties, would have been a natural choice. Moreover, if one *sokaiya* could outmaneuver the other, his reputation would rise to an unimaginable level among *omono sokaiya* ranks.

The Toyo Denki Case

Unlike the Shirokiya dispute, other conflicts were much more straightforward, involving basic payoff schemes made possible because of shareholders' ability to demand explanations and inspect corporate papers and accounting books. The most famous involved the firm, Toyo Denki, or Toyo Electric Company—a case where, at last, a legal position was found regarding the proper use of *sokaiya* in the operation of shareholder meetings.

The incident began in early 1961 when a Tokyo stock-market newspaper reported a rumor that Toyo Denki would soon announce the development of a color television, something no other Japanese television manufacturer had been able to do. From February 1961, the company's share price soared, despite the firm's initial silence about the development. Management's refusal to discuss what would be a major electronics coup for a Japanese company added fuel to the speculative fire. Toyo Denki finally broke its silence in June 1961, displaying the television for the first time at an exhibition in Tokyo. The firm's share price jumped an astounding five hundred yen in a single day. (In Japan, where even today many of the largest and most successful firms have share prices in the five-hundred-yen range, a five-hundred-yen jump in an already soaring stock was unheard of and suggested enormous potential in capital gains for those who could still buy into the stock.) Present at the television's unveiling was its inventor, who attempted to answer attendees' questions. His explanations of the details and how he had developed the television, however, seemed sketchy to some observers. As a result, another rumor spread that the television was just a sham. The company's share price plunged in turn.

On July 28, 1961, at the firm's eighty-sixth regular shareholder meeting, a large number of shareholders demanded that the inventor (who was not at the meeting) and management answer their questions about the color television's development and explain why the share price was allowed to fluctuate so wildly. It was argued that if the television indeed existed, then the company could have stepped in and calmed investor nerves. Shareholders also were skeptical of a second rumor that a special licensing agreement existed that would boost technical development of the television and aid in mass production. They asked to see the alleged agreement, but management was unable to produce it. Eventually, the company's share price dropped two thousand yen. The firm's president resigned to take responsibility and was replaced by the vice president.

The next general shareholders' meeting was on January 30, 1962. Many shareholders held nearly worthless shares after the stock's fall. Management feared investors would take their anger out on them, so police were stationed around the meeting. The new president apologized for the problems in a humiliating display of shame, and the meeting ended shortly thereafter. Most of the shareholders were stunned. They saw this as an amazingly quick settlement of the company's business, given the large issues left unsettled between management who, aside from the former president, were left largely untouched by the scandal, and shareholders, who saw their potential capital gains and some of the principal investment disappear almost overnight.

A new rumor developed: the large fluctuation in the price of the firm's shares was a result of price manipulation. The National Police Agency launched an investigation ten days after the January 1962 shareholder meeting. Their probe revealed that one of the company's directors had bribed *sokaiya* leader Yuzaburo Kubo and another major *sokaiya* to push the July 1961 meeting along as quickly as possible. Before the meeting, Kubo had received seventy thousand yen and the other *sokaiya* had received thirty thousand yen as retainers. Each had then received a hundred thousand yen following the meeting. Moreover, the police learned, prior to the January 1962 meeting, Kubo had received fifty thousand yen and the other *sokaiya* another thirty thousand yen for the same services, and each had received an additional hundred thousand yen following the successful completion of the meeting.

Police charged the director and the two *sokaiya* with violations of Commercial Code Article 494, which prohibited payments in any form in order to influence the exercise of a shareholder's rights to vote. Both parties—those who make such payments and those who receive them—are at fault in such cases. Police and prosecutors argued that such inducements amounted to an "illegal request" (*fusei no seitaku*) and constituted a violation of the Commercial Code. In other words, Toyo Denki had bribed the men to use their shareholder rights to protect the company from questions or arguments. This accusation struck at the heart of the *sokaiya*-management relationship. It did not matter which way the illegal request flowed, from or to *sokaiya*; the request itself was a violation.

The initial court decision, handed down on August 27, 1965, included a detailed analysis of the *sokaiya* position within the Japanese corporate system. It drew a distinction between *sokaiya* and so-called *sokai arashi* (general meeting storm makers). The lower court ruled:

> *Sokaiya* control or own a number of shares in a variety of companies and in answer to requests by these companies work to move along the shareholder meeting. They receive payments which are described as traveling expenses. On the other hand, from other companies, with the intention of receiving payoffs or some kind of profit, *sokai arashi* misuse their status at shareholder meetings to face off against other shareholders, to attack managers for various mistakes, to attack managers for personal mistakes, block the progression of the shareholder meeting by causing a disturbance inside the meeting place, force the com-

pany to recognize them and, under the dint of threats and menace, acquire profits. And then, when the company is found to have a weak point where the shareholder meeting is faced with unavoidable reduction in capital or dividends, they force a clear explanation of all ways money is spent for such things as unsubstantiated expenses, receptions, entertainment costs, etc. To do this they seek to examine all documentation, demanding this be done at the meeting and using this as a threat to extort a large sum of money to maintain silence. (Mitooka 1967, 2–3)

Regarding the defendant Yuzaburo Kubo, the court found:

He is an elder among *sokaiya*, having the confidence of a vast number of *sokaiya* and managing many *sokaiya* himself. From long ago he has received requests from top-ranked, first-section companies to ensure shareholder meetings proceed smoothly.[2] From shareholder meeting managers he receives one-lump payments for his underlings. He distributes this to each underling as a way to ensure countermeasures are developed against the above-mentioned *sokai arashi* and ensures the progress of the meeting without wasted effort. And so, based on the trust of a company's managers or based on his own efforts, he investigates any new shareholders of the company, deals with any newspapers or magazines, gathers information from the financial world and other shareholders and works without pay as a consultant or counselor in which he particularly prides himself. (ibid., 3)

Within this context, the court ruled that

management hired *sokaiya* in order to ensure the proceedings of the meeting and as a defense against *sokai arashi*. This payment for services has to be permitted although a request cannot be permitted in which the speeches of shareholders and the exercising of their rights to vote are blocked. In such a case that type of request would be an illegal request and a violation of the state law (Commercial Code Article 494) and so, given the facts of this case, there is no violation.

Although all defendants were found not guilty, prosecutors appealed the case to the Tokyo High Court (*Tokyo kosai*). (Prosecutors in Japan, unlike prosecutors in the United States, have the right of appeal.) The high court reversed the lower-court ruling on October 17, 1967, finding the defendants guilty of violating Commercial Code Article 494. Moreover, the lower court was taken to task for misinterpreting the code. The high court found that the company and the two *sokaiya* acted in collusion to block questions from shareholders concerning the company's claims about the color television. The company's new president was found negligent in carrying out his responsibilities because he did not acknowledge the problems with the television's development and thus protect the firm's shareholders. As for the two *sokaiya*, they

> did not intend to allow shareholders their legitimate chance to speak or exercise the right to vote, they used their own status as shareholders and abused the rights of a shareholder by planning to forcibly push through management's agenda. That is, in terms of the proceedings of the meeting and pushing those proceedings along, they did not act simply as intermediaries or leaders, but deviated beyond these roles. Thus it is a mistake in reasoning by the lower court that such actions were not seen as unfair.

The high court added that the distinction between *sokaiya* and *sokai arashi* is not pertinent since the law in question was intended to cover the misuse of various shareholder rights:

> The law's legislative objective was the safe exercise of voting rights and discussions in the shareholder meeting. It was also

intended to be applied fairly and impartially. That is to say, whether *sokai arashi*, *sokaiya* or *sokai-goro* [shareholder-meeting ruffians], regardless of whatever name they go by, by utilizing the proper rights of a shareholder, they abuse the shareholder rights (such as the right to speak, ask questions, make proposals, and so on) of others or they somehow hinder other shareholders in the exercise of their proper rights due to a request which involves some sort of profit. This is a violation of Commercial Code Article 494.

The court also found that any distinction between a *sokaiya* or *sokai arashi* was useless since "one company's *sokaiya* can be another's *sokai arashi* or, probably, because of a confrontation with other *sokaiya*, one changes to *sokai arashi* in a given situation. One cannot find a clear basis in fact to make such a distinction" (ibid.).

The 1950s Shirokiya case and the 1960s Toyo Denki case are important signposts of the changed conditions confronting Japanese corporation managers because of the significant redistribution of power resources into the hands of shareholders brought about by Occupation reforms. The ability to examine a firm's books (as in the case of Yokoi and Shirokiya) and threaten reprisals if management made significant errors or violated the trust of investors (as in the Toyo Denki case) represented serious threats to the position of management. More important, it becomes clear how deeply *sokaiya* penetrated to all levels of the management process, serving as intermediaries as well as management mercenaries. In spite of fundamental changes, then, *sokaiya*, like other criminal organizations, were able to adapt or turn to their own advantage any changes in the basic structure of the system within which they operate.

Yakuza Penetration

The deep base of trust between managers and *sokaiya* is plain. However, even as these events were taking place, others were occurring that would introduce new blood into the *sokaiya* field and radically alter the structure of the *sokaiya*-management relationship. In particular, the relationship among members of mainstream organized-crime groups (*yakuza*), radical-right-wing political groups (*uyoku-ha*), the ruling Liberal Democratic Party (LDP), and the bureaucracy was undergoing a fundamental change.

Central to this discussion is the radical-right-wing leader, Yoshio Kodama, who was active in the politically volatile decades of the 1950s and 1960s. He was instrumental in breaking the back of left-wing challenges to the government by using ultranationalists and gangsters to suppress protestors opposed to the first U.S.–Japan security pact in 1960. He was already a well-known figure in the back rooms and back-alley manipulations of government power. He had worked for the Japanese government during World War II in Shanghai and remained active after the war with the new Japanese government and the Allied occupiers. As the day of the security-pact signing approached in June 1960, Japanese officials were concerned about the anti-pact protests. It was feared the fifteen-thousand-member Tokyo police force would be too small to control the crowd. Kodama promised the officials he would deliver some sixty thousand gangsters and rightists who would work with the police to combat the protesters. The protests proved large and the street fighting bloody. Then-President Dwight Eisenhower canceled his trip to Tokyo for the signing because of the violence. Still, the pact was signed and order was maintained. Kodama's ability to amass large numbers of reliable thugs was greatly appreciated. With his action, he cemented his position as an offstage political power. But there were unintended consequences to his action; most notably, he unknowingly set the stage for a mass influx of *yakuza* into *sokaiya* ranks.

In December 1963, three years after his antiprotest success, Kodama established the *Toa Doyu-kai* or East Asia Comrades Association. This was a powerful grouping of seven criminal and ultranationalist organizations operating in the Tokyo metropolitan area that included Kinsei-kai, Sumiyoshi-kai, Matsuba-kai, Nippon Kokusui-kai, Nippon Gijinto, Hoikusei-kai, and Tosei-kai. Kodama's stated purpose for the association was that it would stand ready to defend the government if threatened by a coup from the Left. Toa Doyu-kai thus represented a powerful force of politically reliable violent groups operating under a single umbrella organization that could provide informal private-security services to the government.

Immediately following the establishment of Toa Doyu-kai, Kodama sent a letter to the upper- and lower-house Diet members (similar to senators and representatives in the U.S. Congress) of the LDP. The letter was signed not only by Kodama, but by the leaders of the Toa Doyu-kai groups as well. In it, they demanded that party members cease factional infighting, arguing that such political wrangling deflected attention from the business of governing the state, thereby weakening the LDP and allowing subversive elements to grow in strength. LDP leaders were shocked not only by Kodama's arrogance in attempting to interfere in party affairs, but also at the signatures of political extremists and gangsters on the letter.

The politicians, recognizing the powerful threat Toa Doyu-kai represented, retreated from full contact with Kodama. In March 1964, the National Police Agency established a new headquarters to handle investigations of organized-crime groups (Katzenstein and Tsujinaka 1991, 32). They followed this in 1965 with the first major postwar campaign against the *yakuza*, involving the arrest and imprisonment of top organized-crime leaders. Two similar campaigns followed, in 1969 and 1975, but the first crackdown had already effectively shifted the political leaders' view of organized crime and the radical right from that of a reliable ally to a significant threat. Of course, the politicians did not fear a coup. Instead, they were concerned about public visibility of what had been a private arrangement. The potential for scandal was too great. But these crackdowns had another effect that was unintended.

As police pressure increased on crime groups throughout the latter half of the 1960s, the groups began moving more deeply into *sokaiya* activities. Not only were *yakuza* turning to new careers as *sokaiya*, but their organizations were acting as supporters of existing *sokaiya* groups, lending muscle when needed. Part of this movement was the brainchild of Kodama, who, police reported, linked his efforts to *sokaiya* as a source of continued funding for his own operations. Kodama, according to one writer, shared leadership in the *sokaiya* world with Giichi Miura, another ultrarightist. The two, it was said, split *sokaiya* operations between them to avoid territorial disputes (Inoue 1966, 59).

If such were the case, Kodama's timing could not have been better. By the late 1960s, the major prewar *sokaiya* leaders were either retiring, dead, or relatively ineffective figureheads. Younger and more aggressive individuals jockeyed for top positions through new tactics. They were not like the older leaders, known as "lone wolves," who, through reputation and a few trusted backers, could control a meeting and face off against other *sokaiya*. The new rising *sokaiya* stars, even with *yakuza* backing, could not depend on reputation alone because they were still too new. Corporate managers did not know them, their strengths, or weaknesses. So a new philosophy developed by the end of the 1960s and the early 1970s, based on "numbers and violence" (*kazu to boryoku*). In other words, through mass attendance at meetings, the ability to call on *yakuza* groups for additional muscle, and a willingness to use that muscle in or out of a shareholder meeting, the new *sokaiya* could come to dominate the world of the old where, for decades (according to police and *sokaiya* sources), a few hundred *sokaiya* operated in all of Japan.

The source of the numbers-and-violence philosophy is attributed to Kaoru Ogawa, a prominent gangster in the Hiroshima area linked with *Kyosei-kai*, the dominant organized-crime group in that city. As with other such groups, the police crackdown on Kyosei-kai disrupted chains of command and sources of funding. Ogawa seized the chance to move into the open territory of the *sokaiya*, forming what would become known as the Hiroshima Group (*Hiroshima gurupu*) and operating throughout Japan with the backing of Kyosei-kai leaders.

The first known confrontation between Ogawa and an old-style *sokaiya*, Eiji Shimazaki, took place in November 1971 at the shareholder meeting of Oji Paper Company, held in the Marunouchi section of central Tokyo and attended by some two hundred shareholders. Shimazaki held up the meeting with a long series of questions about management policy. Ogawa and one of his partners approached Shimazaki, requesting that he "hold on." A young member of Shimazaki's group became incensed at this disrespect toward his leader and attacked Ogawa, thus beginning a wild free-for-all in the meeting hall. One witness, knowledgeable about the *sokaiya* world, commented: "This was the beginning of the end of the well-disciplined methods of the *sokaiya*. The Oji Paper shareholders meeting served as the stage for the beginning of a face-off between the old and new style *sokaiya*" ("Zoka suru Boryoku-sokaiya no gokuhi risuto o hatsukokai" 1978, 83).

Had this been the only confrontation between old and new *sokaiya* groups, it might have had as little significance as the proverbial new kid on the block challenging the neighborhood bully—frightening and disruptive, perhaps, but hardly noteworthy. However, what made it more than a simple confrontation among *sokaiya* was a meeting that took place later at a Tokyo hotel, where Shimazaki and Ogawa performed a reconciliation ceremony, or *teuchishiki*.

At the meeting, Shimazaki was backed by Norikatsu Kikuchi, a former leader within Matsuba-kai, one of the seven groups involved in Kodama's Toa Doyu-kai organization. By this time the organization had disbanded, but it remained a historic symbol of power of Matsuba-kai's influence in the Tokyo region. Kyosei-kai, the Hiroshima gangster organization, sent its main leader, Takeshi Hattori, to stand by Ogawa, thus demonstrating the importance of the meeting (something less significant, and Hattori would have sent a representative). Witnesses said Matsuba-kai counselor (*komon*) Kotaro Kuno made the following reconciliation speech: "As there are territorial disputes among *yakuza*, there are territorial disputes among *sokaiya*. It is better for both sides to let bygones be bygones; water over the dam" (ibid., 84).

The ceremony struck at the heart of the old-style leadership. *Yakuza* were no longer content to be mere bystanders in *sokaiya* matters. Rather, they now served as intermediaries and conciliators, lending their own names and power—and that of their organizations—to the settlement of a dispute among *sokaiya*. Ogawa had effectively propelled himself into the ranks of the prominent new *sokaiya* with a single, well-timed move at a shareholder meeting. He had forced Shimazaki, one of the most powerful old-style *sokaiya* leaders of the late 1960s and 1970s, to recognize his importance in the field, and Shimazaki, in turn, was himself forced to rely on *yakuza* backing to settle a dispute.

So within a few decades following World War II, the face of corporate Japan changed, thanks to new conditions imposed by Occupation reformers. With new or revised laws, *sokaiya* and others could directly challenge corporate managers. Some *sokaiya* found themselves to be more necessary than ever to the maintenance of management control of their firm. Political changes, too, forced organized-crime groups to seek new sources of funding due to police crackdowns on more traditional *yakuza* operations. The movement into *sokaiya* activities was a natural redirection of resources. Moreover, the new *yakuza-sokaiya*, while less skilled perhaps than their more traditional predecessors, forced new alliances which raised the threat of violence and intimidation to a new level at the shareholder meeting and within *sokaiya* ranks.

All of this allowed the new generation of *sokaiya* to cement relations with management as new challenges to corporate power arose. While Commercial Code knowledge was still important, the instrumental violence of the *yakuza* would become ever more necessary to combat these challenges.

Notes

1. The descriptions of early *sokaiya* were compiled from Ito 1966, 50–51; Kawamoto and Monma 1976, 181–82; and Minato 1979. Additional information was gathered from one of the few books authored by a *sokaiya*, Yuzaburo Kubo's *Sokaiya gojyunen* (Fifty Years of *Sokaiya*).

2. The Tokyo, Osaka, and Nagoya stock exchanges divide companies into two tiers or "sections."

3

Conflict, Resolution, Adaptation

For those seemingly few socially aware Japanese in the early 1970s, death seemed to ooze from the smokestacks and waste pipes of corporate Japan. After decades of rapid development, the streams and rivers near the urban and manufacturing centers of Japan were little more than foul sewers, nearly devoid of life. Any chemical that could not be burned off into the air could be buried in the ground or pumped into the water. Few cared. Production was not only necessary, it was a virtue—and, with some of Japan's products making their way to Vietnam to be used as weapons of war, it was also profitable. This attitude of indifference changed, however, when the effects of such unchecked production and pollution began to have a tangible impact on people's lives. And yet corporate Japan refused to accept the reality. Indeed, rather than heed the calls for reform, it unleashed the one weapon at its disposal: *sokaiya*.

This chapter will look at how the social problems of pollution and, to a lesser extent, Japan's corporate involvement in the war in Vietnam revealed extensively and publicly the linkage between company management and *sokaiya* groups. The resulting conflict eventually required a resolution as government officials, including police and politicians, and the news media demanded some sort of reform that would break corporation ties to *sokaiya*. As we have already seen, however, the necessity for *sokaiya* services led to new adaptations by corporations and *sokaiya*.

The Minamata Protests

In the 1950s, the people of Minamata, a small fishing village on Kyushu, the southernmost of Japan's four main islands, began to experience an unusually high number of birth defects. The villagers blamed Chisso Corporation, which had been producing fertilizer at its plant upriver from Minamata since before World War II. Mercury was a main catalyst in the production process; once used, it was then dumped into the waters around Minamata, where it contaminated the shellfish and fish consumed by the villagers. The results: horrific birth defects and severe neurological damage (McKean 1981, 50). Some reports indicate that as many as 40 percent of the victims died from the condition soon known as "Minamata disease." All the while, Chisso executives attempted to quiet any protest, refused to take responsibility for the pollution problem, but did agree to make small "sympathy payments" instead of compensation payments. This allowed the corporation to buy out some protesters without ever agreeing to take on responsibility for the problem (Upham 1987, 30–33).

The birth defects and the denial by Chisso that it was to blame for them led to a number of confrontations. Some of these took place in court when lawsuits by the victims were filed in 1967.

But the victims and their families soon grew impatient with what they saw as a never-ending process of argument and counterargument in court.

One of the other resources available to the victims and their supporters was public denunciation at shareholder meetings. The victims began using tactics that soon became known as the "One-Share Stockholder Movement" (*hitokabu kabunushi undo*, OSSM).

Unlike Westerners, the Japanese do not routinely practice the public airing of disputes, believing polite discussion compels clashing parties to maintain at least a semblance of mutual goodwill and understanding. The threat of exposure and shame are just beneath the surface of the discussion. At stake is the accused party's reputation, and any threat of damage to that reputation is an effective sanction in Japan—more effective than the threat of a lawsuit (Haley 1982, 280). Experts have noted that conflict in Japan "is not considered natural; rather, it is regarded as an embarrassment to be avoided whenever possible" (Krauss, Rohlen, and Steinhoff 1984, 11).

That is not to say, however, that litigation—which some Japanese believe is a Western disease—is not an option. Indeed, as we have seen, Minamata victims and other pollution victims engaged in several major lawsuits involving their cause. Depending on the circumstances, however, litigation is not always the most effective weapon. As Haley points out, few incentives exist for becoming involved in a lawsuit in Japan:

> The continental system of disconnected hearings, trials *de novo* upon first appeal, the appeal of right to the Supreme Court rather than by court of discretion, filing fees, bond posting requirements, stringent requirements of evidentiary proof, the unwillingness of judges to discipline lawyers for unnecessary delays— all combine to foreclose the courts as a viable means of obtaining relief. (Haley 1982, 274)

Public confrontation was not a new strategy at the time of the Minamata conflict. *Burakumin* (social outcasts) had used confrontation or denunciation (*kyudan*) since the 1920s and, following World War II, defended its use as a right guaranteed by the new postwar constitution. Denunciation, where those accused of discrimination are targeted for confrontation, gave *burakumin* leaders "greater control over the course and outcome of conflict than they would have enjoyed had they relied on the judiciary" (Upham 1987, 24). Pharr (1990) notes that confrontation by what she terms "status inferiors" (those of lower social status) with "status superiors" is not limited to the *burakumin* movement. After describing the use of similar strategies by samurai in the feudal era and by young military officers in the twentieth century, she links the use of the *kyudan* technique to other status-inferior protests as well:

> Key writers and activists of the Buraku Liberation League [a major *burakumin* organization] hold that although the Burakumin learned many methods from other protest movements, such as those of farmers and labor in the 1920s, they themselves refined the technique and used the term "kyudan" for the first time. . . . It is no surprise, then, that the kyudan method forged by Burakumin bears distinct similarities to the confrontation, accusatory approach used by peasant groups in some of the *ikki* (uprisings) of the Tokugawa era. (Pharr 1990, 128–29)

In the Minamata case, victims based their claim to public confrontation on the right of the owner of a single share of company stock to confront the corporation's board of directors with complaints and questions about management. Legally, they were on solid ground, and the tactic was also effective at a simple and emotional level. Because victims and supporters each had bought a single share of Chisso stock, they were granted access to the firm's shareholder meetings. Once there, the victims peppered the board with questions about compensation as well as corporate social responsibility. Witnesses recall: "The victims waved their malformed limbs only inches away from the eyes of executives of the polluting company. . . . Mothers held up their children, malformed and shaking with spasms, immediately in front of the officials' faces. But those faces remained totally impassive and silent. At some point an executive would be overcome by it all and faint, a loyal servant of his company to the last" (Van Wolferen 1989, 336).

The confrontations were a public relations nightmare. The news media fed on images of pain-racked, horribly deformed victims asking questions. Eventually Eugene Smith, a photographer for *Life* magazine, covered the victims' plight, and his pictures focused international attention on the victims. The power of confrontation through denunciation was revealed as the company struggled to cope with the onslaught of bad publicity and the threat to its already damaged reputation.

The protesters insisted they were not interested in payoffs. "The victims and others took up the motto that 'We don't want even one sen [a fraction of a yen]. What we want is for the executives of the company to drink a glass of mercury" (Minato 1979, 222). Since management was insisting that mercury was not a cause of harm, they either wanted direct proof or to have management assume full responsibility for the pollution and its effects.

Management, however, had its own ways of dealing with the protests at shareholder meetings. Chisso hired *sokaiya* groups who, armed with their own shares, shouted down the victims and demanded that meetings be brought to a quick conclusion (something the directors could not do themselves). The frustration and persistence of the protesters led to physical violence inside and outside the meeting rooms, with fights involving the victims, their supporters, *sokaiya*, company personnel, and security guards hired to bolster corporate ranks.

In the end, the victims believed the OSSM tactic to be successful in spite of their physical injuries and their inability to move management away from its position—not because it forced the company to capitulate, as this did not happen, but because it brought pressure and attention on the corporation, neither of which it wanted. Victims argued that they were able to demonstrate just how unreasonable and unfeeling management really was.

The Antiwar Protests

At the same time the Minamata drama played on, a second stream of anticorporate social activism using the OSSM strategy cropped up among antiwar protesters locked in a struggle against Japanese corporate and government support of the profiteering from the Vietnam War. The group that made particular use of the OSSM tactic was Beheiren (*Betonamu heiwa rengo*, or Peace for Vietnam Committee). Organized in 1965 as a "spontaneous alliance of people [opposed to] the impersonality of huge organizations, public or private, labor or corporate, Beheiren saw the Vietnam War as a symbol of the evils produced by contemporary bureaucracies: anonymous warfare, in direction and execution, by the Americans and constant complicity by a monolithic Japanese state" (Havens 1987, 57–58).

Beheiren members began using the OSSM tactic in 1971. One of the most detailed accounts involved the shareholder meeting of Mitsubishi Heavy Industries. In May 1971, a phalanx of 250 chanting antiwar shareholders wearing death-head masks sporting the three-diamond symbol of Mitsubishi, descended on the meeting at Hibiya Public Hall in Tokyo. There, outside the meeting hall, they encountered a wall of *sokaiya*, ultranationalists, special company-hired security guards, and company employees. The protesters managed to fight their way inside both times, only to face more violence from company forces. *Sokaiya* and ultranationalists blocked Beheiren speakers from floor microphones and beat those who resisted. The questions of other protesters were ignored. *Sokaiya* made motions, quickly passed, to close the meetings (Baldwin 1974, 504–5; Berg and Berg 1971, 54–55).

As in the Minamata case, company policy was never directly affected, and Mitsubishi and other corporations targeted by Beheiren continued providing supplies for U.S. military forces in Vietnam. However, Beheiren members, like the Minamata pollution victims, nevertheless claimed victory, saying they had exposed the brutality of the corporation and its willingness to flout the law by its open refusal to recognize what the protesters considered legitimate shareholder claims. Groups associated with Beheiren used the OSSM tactic at a number of other firms, and some eventually were branded "leftist *sokaiya*" by the media as the ground war in Vietnam dissipated, but their protests against corporations remained strident (Shiso undo kenkyujo 1972, 388–89).

In the end, whatever claims the Minamata and Beheiren supporters might have regarding the net effect of their protests, these challenges to Japan's corporate system, and to management's efforts to maintain direct control of the corporation, remain a watershed in Japan's postwar corporate history. They revealed that the shareholder meeting, outwardly the highest organ in the corporate decision-making process since shareholders are in fact owners of the company, left the corporation terribly exposed to outside criticism by those very same owners. The threat of damage to reputation—especially corporate reputation—was the most feared of all sanctions, and the shareholder meeting was at least one place where the corporation's reputation was exposed to outside harm.

There is a second reason that the protests are a watershed for corporate Japan. They proved beyond doubt that *sokaiya* were a necessary part of corporate security. In the midst of the protests, management had to assure itself of a dependable security force that would break the law to serve the interests of management. This provided a larger way in for would-be *sokaiya* who, if they could not receive payments for protecting a company, knew that firms were particularly sensitive to outside threats at this time of social unrest. Consequently, as we will see, the *sokaiya* population mushroomed.

Further *Yakuza* Penetration

Long-time *sokaiya* leader Eiji Shimazaki (see chapter 2) was the man in charge of defending both Chisso and Mitsubishi in the fight against the OSSM opposition. To do so, he drew upon his affiliation with organized-crime syndicates, relying on right-wing groups and *yakuza* to supply the extra manpower necessary to fend off mass protests outside and inside the shareholder meetings. Whereas a handful of men could manipulate the more normal disruptions at a meeting, the protests put a strain on regular *sokaiya* forces. *Yakuza* groups were willing to join Shimazaki's efforts. But there were others who formed their own groups and conducted their own operations independently of old-line *sokaiya* leaders such as Shimazaki. Like the Hiroshima Group, which was formed by Kaoru Ogawa and traced its roots to the Kyosei-kai gangster organization of that city, other major organized-crime groups had established their own *sokaiya* rackets by the late 1960s, expanding during the 1970s.

In 1978, for the first time, the National Police Agency (NPA) reported its estimate of the *sokaiya* population in its annual white paper on police and crime activities. These papers, published annually since 1973, are similar to the Uniform Crime Reports published by the U.S. Federal Bureau of Investigation in that they offer a variety of statistics and explanations about crimes committed, police responses to those crimes, details about police activities, and short reports on such issues as radicals on the Left and Right. Usually, the small section on *sokaiya* is contained within the larger section dealing with organized crime.

In the 1978 white paper, police presented a situation that was clearly out of control. A decade earlier there had been perhaps only a few hundred *sokaiya* throughout the nation; by 1975, according to the police, the *sokaiya* population stood at 5,227. The following year the population jumped by more than one thousand to 6,240, and in 1977 the number again increased, to 6,504. An estimated 10 percent (about 650) of these *sokaiya*, the police agency reported, were actually members of known *yakuza* organizations (National Police Agency 1978, 134).

The NPA reasoned that the potential for easy profits was one of the main reasons *yakuza* entered into the *sokaiya* field. In 1974, police reported confiscating some 900 million yen (about $2.5 million) from those involved in corporate extortion and *sokaiya* businesses. In the same year, arrests of *yakuza* yielded confiscations of some 8.6 billion yen from drug sales, 3.8 billion yen from gambling, 300 million yen from prostitution, and 200 million yen from pornography. Clearly, the confiscated profits from *sokaiya* protection rackets were outpacing two of the main sources of organized crime income—prostitution and pornography. Of course, these are confiscated profits, so they do not give an accurate picture of how much money is actually earned in these pursuits. Moreover, confiscations of profits may be affected by the police focusing on a particular kind of crime (e.g., more focus on extortion and less on pornography) or unusually large confiscations beyond what would be average. There is no average provided and no real estimate of profits from extortion is available, although the NPA did admit that the actual income from all sources was yielding ten times the figures presented—figures that represented confiscated money only. There was no explanation of how police arrived at that estimate (National Police Agency 1978, 130).

Far more important, police and others observers noted, was that the penetration of the *sokaiya* field by *yakuza* groups was a disturbing trend in terms of economic crimes. Unlike prostitution, gambling, or drugs, *yakuza* working the *sokaiya* milieu gained access to the heart of Japan's corporate world—a corporate world that, because of its "peace-at-any-price philosophy" (*kotonagare-shugi*), paid well to silence scandal and dissent. *Sokaiya* operations were particularly attractive to *yakuza* because they were safer; corporate executives were unlikely to call in police and risk further scandal or the discovery of illegal practices (Nakabayashi 1978, 656; National Police Agency 1978, 130). A *sokaiya*—*yakuza* or otherwise—could earn a sizeable income once he attained a high rank and a reputation for effective handling of corporate problems, or a readiness to do violence.

However, amassing large cash payoffs from corporations was not the only way *yakuza* groups earned money from *sokaiya* rackets; they also counted on protection money from *sokaiya* themselves. Both Ogawa and Shimazaki paid heavy premiums for the backing they received from mainstream *yakuza* groups. Shimazaki, who brought backers from Matsuba-kai to his reconciliation meeting with Ogawa (see chapter 2), established ties to at least six other large *yakuza* organizations, including Yamaguchi-gumi and Sumiyoshi Rengo—at that time, the nation's largest and second-largest criminal syndicates respectively. Shimazaki allegedly paid some 50 million yen per year for these protective and supportive services ("Zoka suru Boryoku-sokaiya no gokuhi risuto o hatsukokai" 1978, 85).

In the late 1970s, the respected business magazine *Shukan daiyamondo* published charts showing known connections between *sokaiya* and gangster organizations as well as gangster organizations running their own *sokaiya* groups. That is, the *sokaiya* leaders were not themselves *yakuza*, but through necessity, desire, or circumstance, they established a working relationship with these criminal syndicates. One theory holds that those groups that were once part of the Yoshio Kodama–inspired Toa Doyu-kai (see chapter 2) gained entry into *sokaiya* operations through connections between Kodama, his own links to corporations, and corporations' connections to *sokaiya*. However, other methods of growing within the *sokaiya* profession existed.

During the 1970s, *yakuza* leaders sent a steady stream of capable, mid-level members of their own crime organizations to apprentice with the mainstream *sokaiya*. Under the tutelage of *sokaiya* leaders, *yakuza* apprentices gained valuable insider knowledge about corporate management and manipulative techniques. Further, the threat to use such information could be more effective than the overt threat of physical harm. After several years of training, these so-called *yakuza-sokaiya* established their own groups. In effect, *yakuza* were becoming less dependent on mainstream *sokaiya* for entry into the corporate world. By 1978, according to the National Police Agency, *yakuza* earned an estimated 42 billion yen through their own *sokaiya* operations or through tribute payments from mainstream *sokaiya*—reputedly 4.7 percent of the combined annual earnings of all *yakuza* syndicates (National Police Agency 1979, 129).

Among these *yakuza-sokaiya* organizations are also pseudo right-wing groups (*ese uyoku dantai*), including Nippon Seishikai, Nippon Kokuseidan Suisennin, and Aikoku Seinen Hyogi-kai. During Japan's early postwar years, the right wing was deeply involved in the suppression of dissent and threats to the status quo such as the street fighting they engaged in against protesters of the 1960 U.S.–Japan security treaty and the smashing of a labor dispute at Mitsubishi's Miike coal mine a few years earlier. They, along with mainstream *yakuza* organizations, acted as an informal supplemental police force for the government which lacked adequate riot-control units until the Metropolitan Police Department (MPD), Japan's official riot police, was established in 1954. By the late 1950s, the MPD had only approximately 1,800 riot police in the country (Katzenstein and Tsujinaka 1991, 60–61).

Politicians, bureaucrats, and corporate executives were keenly sensitive to the issues raised by the right wing, either because they supported the issues themselves and were therefore willing to support right-wing positions, or because they feared being seen as willing to ignore traditional beliefs and values. Gangster organizations found that the use of right-wing rhetoric to attack an individual or corporation was an extremely effective tool in extortion rackets. In addition, the constitutional rights of free political thought and expression provided the right-wing immediate protection from police interference. Blatant acts of harassment and intimidation were committed by the pseudo right wing under the guise of political protests. (See Nihon Bengoshi Rengokai 1986; Takagi 1989; and Szymkowiak and Steinhoff 1995 for detailed analyses of the use of the right-wing cover to perpetrate criminal activities.)

Anti-*Sokaiya* Protection Groups

In the mid-1970s the National Police Agency began touting a new cooperative effort in which local police worked with groups of corporations to form anti-*sokaiya* protective associations. The timing was good, with companies reeling from reduced incomes due to the oil embargo imposed by the Organization of Petroleum Exporting Countries—meaning companies had less money for payoffs. The weakened financial situation hit firms at about the same time public criticism against corrupt or antisocial practices by firms increased. This was highlighted by the collusion between politicians and corporate managers in the Lockheed and Grumman payoff scandals, which involved payment of millions of dollars to politicians in order to guarantee the awarding of lucrative aircraft-construction contracts. Again, Yoshio Kodama was the focus; he had served as intermediary between U.S. corporations and Japanese politicians (Mae 1977, 35).

By 1978 the NPA had helped establish twelve protection groups with a total membership of 798 companies in Tokyo alone. Another 345 companies formed alliances in Osaka, and similar associations appeared in Kyoto, Fukuoka, and Yokohama (National Police Agency 1979, 129). The protection associations went by a variety of names but were generically known as "independent support groups," or *jishu bogyo dantai*. NPA, local police officials, and top corporate managers discussed ways to block *sokaiya* advances and traded information about various *sokaiya*. When police officials informed a group that a *sokaiya* had been arrested or was under investigation, they used the information as a pretext to announce that member firms would no longer make payoffs to that *sokaiya*.

The first support group in Osaka was established on June 27, 1975, and involved representatives from eighty-five securities companies, financial institutions, pharmaceutical companies, trading companies, and other firms headquartered in the four-square-kilometer area of Senba, the business district of Osaka. The group initially called itself the Round-Table Committee on the Elimination of Violence Against Companies (Kaisha boryoku haijo kondankai), but formally changed its name in September 1975 to the Eastern Precinct Enterprise Protection Association (Higashi shokannai kigyo boei taisaku kyogikai). Yoshio Otaguro, the general affairs chief of Sumitomo Bank, was the group's leader (Mae 1977, 34).

The association established five aims:

1. Stronger mutual understanding and cooperation between police and corporations.
2. The division of the Senba business area into four sections, each with its own area committee.
3. Further discussion between police and member corporations within each area committee.
4. Establishment of measures to deal with *sokaiya* that met the needs of members within each area.
5. Respect for and cooperation with the execution of all measures agreed upon by each area committee.

The group first eliminated all support payments (*sanjokin*) to new *sokaiya* (those who had previously not operated in the area). The measures were put to an immediate test when a *yakuza*-linked right-wing group was designated as the first to be denied support payments. On September 16, 1975, after racketeers carried out a series of violent acts against local corporations, the corporate-protection association voted to end all payoffs to them. The police then took action by visiting the offices of the right-wing group's leader, explaining the action of the association and informing the leader that the police would enforce the measure in cooperation with the member firms (ibid.).

It is not known what the actual outcome of this effort was or how the right-wing group's leader reacted, but there was apparent success. The protection association decided that even greater efforts could be tried, involving the distribution among member firms of written information about various *sokaiya*, more active participation by police in visiting those *sokaiya* deemed particularly troublesome by the association, and the decision to end corporate participation in *sokaiya*-sponsored golf competitions, parties, seminars, and anniversary celebrations. In the past, *sokaiya* and corporations had used such events to circumvent Article 494 of the Commercial Code which prohibited payoffs involving illegal requests. Asking a firm to participate in a golf tournament or help sponsor a seminar would hardly be construed as an illegal request (except for the implicit threat if the firm did not participate). Entry fees and other payments, which appeared as legitimate corporate activities on corporate account records, provided an easy method for the transfer of payoffs to *sokaiya* groups.

In October 1975 in addition to the efforts by the corporations, the local police established a special investigative unit in Osaka to target *sokaiya* activities and make arrests. Officers from this unit met face-to-face with corporate managers, asking them to end their association with *sokaiya*. In one instance, top officials from the National Police Agency attended a meeting of the directors of the Japan Federation of Bankers Association (Zenkoku kingo kyokai rengokai) who represented the most powerful financial associations in the nation. Police asked that banks dissociate themselves from *sokaiya* and cooperate with the police, as banks—which have always valued their public image for probity—were a major source of corporate payoffs to *sokaiya*.

Those firms eager to reduce payoffs to racketeers were watchful of the Osaka experiment. By the end of 1982, when a reformed Commercial Code was about to take effect, some 2,877 companies were part of independent protection associations in forty-four municipalities, representing nearly all corporations that were listed on the nation's stock exchanges and that were therefore also potential targets of *sokaiya* extortion rackets (National Police Agency 1983, 111).

As the numbers of protective groups grew, they also grew in boldness. For example, in 1978, associations across the nation collectively decided to cut all payments to *sokaiya* by a uniform 20 percent. Whether these were actual cuts, how much these cuts represented in terms of actual loss of income by *sokaiya*, and whether or not *sokaiya* were in some way reimbursed for these cuts through other methods is largely unknown but, as we will see, efforts apparently continued which ensured a stream of funds to *sokaiya* (Mae 1977, 35; Nakabayashi 1978, 656).

Yet the question remains: Did the cooperative efforts of police and corporations have any effect on *sokaiya*? Annual arrest reports found in police white papers may not be of much help since, like much crime data around the world, they reveal only what the police wish to disclose. The reports merely reflect the number of persons arrested for extortion or other violent activities; they do not show the effectiveness of the protective association programs or demonstrate the degree of increase or decrease in *sokaiya* activity. Further, they do not indicate changes in the number of contacts or incidents between *sokaiya* and corporations. In any case, an analysis of population and arrest data does show a steady increase in the number of arrests. In 1975 there were an estimated 5,227 *sokaiya* operating in Japan. Of those, one hundred or about 1.91 percent of the *sokaiya* population were arrested. By 1977, when the number of protective associations was growing, police reported that the estimated *sokaiya* population was 6,504, and 419 *sokaiya* (6.44 percent) were arrested. Two years later, in 1981, the police believed 6,309 *sokaiya* were active, and they arrested 499 of them or 7.9 percent. Thus, there did seem to be an effect from the increased cooperation between police and corporations.

Shareholder-Meeting Operations

Better indicators of *sokaiya* activity are statistics concerning any changes in the conduct of corporate shareholder meetings. Requests and demands for payoffs, or planning sessions between *sokaiya* and managers can take place behind closed doors or in private meetings at restaurants, for example. Shareholder meetings are the one place where *sokaiya* activity is clearly revealed. The authoritative legal journal *Shoji homu* (Legal Affairs) annually reports the results of a survey conducted by its staff about the running of shareholder meetings around the nation. The survey is sent to all corporations on the nation's stock exchanges. Since 1972, when the first survey in the annual series was conducted, it has been the only important resource for any analysis of shareholder-meeting activities in Japan.

Before analyzing the *Shoji homu* survey results, it should be noted that at least one survey was conducted prior to *Shoji homu*'s annual effort. In 1965, 387 companies were asked by the Tokyo Stock Exchange about conditions of their general shareholder meetings (Kawamoto and Monma 1976, 184). In that survey, 382 firms reported holding shareholder meetings lasting one hour or less, with the vast majority (80 percent) running under thirty minutes. Attendance was also startlingly low: ninety out of 320 companies responding to that question reported more than a hundred people in attendance, while 106 companies reported fifty to one hundred people and 124 firms said fewer than fifty people came to the shareholder meeting.

There are a number of reasons for ending shareholder meetings quickly, not all of them involving *sokaiya*. For example, there are few individual shareholders, since more than 75 percent of shares traded on the Japanese stock market are held by large companies and financial institutions. Hence there is no need to raise questions, as long as these private investors receive a respectable return on their investments. Further, many shareholders prefer to cast their votes through proxies instead of concerning themselves with the affairs of the corporation, again in anticipation of a return on their investments (ibid., 184–85).

The 1965 survey served as a baseline and a model for the *Shoji homu* series. With the start of the series of surveys we begin to gain a more accurate picture of Japanese corporate governance. If the efforts by protective associations and police were having an effect, then answers to specific questions about *sokaiya* operations and the workings of the shareholder meetings should reveal that effect. I will analyze the answers to each question based on data from the *Shoji homu* surveys.

Did Shareholder Meetings Grow Longer?

Shareholder-meeting length in Japan is usually quite short, despite the fact that a company's affairs are supposed to be examined and discussed by shareholders prior to approval of any bills or policy changes. *Sokaiya* are often hired by companies to silence shareholders and push through management's agenda; hence short meetings could indicate some collusion between *sokaiya* and management. On the other hand, long meetings could indicate that *sokaiya* targeted the meeting for disruption, perhaps as a way to extract future payoffs, or in retaliation for not receiving payoffs or for receiving payoffs they viewed as insufficient. The answers, of course, are not stated directly in the survey responses. The survey does not ask for an explanation of why meetings ran long or short. However, in theory, the running time of meetings should grow longer if less money is being paid or if *sokaiya* are being cut off and companies are engaging in active resistance through cooperation with police. In other words, the meetings would grow longer because *sokaiya* would be forced to raise the stakes with management in order to force management to make payments.

The majority of Japanese companies (91.4 percent) surveyed from 1971 through 1981 held meetings lasting no longer than thirty minutes. Most meetings during these years (55.35 percent) lasted between fifteen and thirty minutes. When compared over time, the length of meetings on a year-to-year basis changed relatively little. There was a slight upward movement in 1975, when the companies and police began developing the group-protection programs in earnest. However, this increase may also be due to the effects of the oil embargo, when Japanese companies had to tighten their belts and reduce some payments to *sokaiya*.

Following six years of the group-protection program, combined with increased police arrests and investigative efforts, more—not fewer—meetings were still running at thirty minutes or less. Moreover, the number of meetings running from thirty-one minutes to an hour fell from 6.2 percent in 1971 to 4.1 percent in 1981. One might conclude, therefore, that *sokaiya* were still active in pushing through meeting agendas and that companies likely still were in collusion with *sokaiya* in spite of the outward appearance of cooperation with police. It is in the company's interest to maintain a good image and run meetings quickly (under a half hour). If *sokaiya* were feeling threatened about losing income, they would ensure disruptions at as many meetings as possible to make meetings run as long as possible.

Did the Number of Sokaiya *Known to Companies Decrease or Increase?*

Theoretically, the number of *sokaiya* known to companies would decrease over time, as *sokaiya* operations became more difficult to conduct in the face of police-corporation anti-*sokaiya* efforts. *Sokaiya* might respond to police action and corporate resistance by concentrating greater efforts on fewer corporations. In fact, this seems to have been the case. The percentage of companies reporting no contact with *sokaiya* grew from 2.1 percent in 1975 (the year this data was first reported) to 4.1 percent by 1981. *Sokaiya* were apparently targeting certain companies, as an increasing number of firms were reporting more contacts with between 101 and more than five hundred *sokaiya*. In other words, a small number of companies was being left alone while a greater number was being flooded with new contacts by *sokaiya*. Thus while police action and group-protection associations seemed to have some beneficial effect for a small group of firms, a growing number of companies was being targeted by more and more *sokaiya*.

Did the Number of Sokaiya *Attending Meetings Change?*

There is apparently no significant change in the number of *sokaiya* attending shareholder meetings after 1975, although one element should be noted. The percentage of companies reporting no *sokaiya* in attendance rose from 8.3 percent in 1975 to 11.7 percent in 1981 (a nearly 30 percent increase). However, this may be due to more *sokaiya* turning up at fewer meetings, since the percentage of companies reporting eleven or more *sokaiya* in attendance jumped from 35.7 percent in 1975 to 40.8 percent in 1976. This change in attendance patterns probably reflects the unintended consequences of the policy adopted by the protection associations in the late 1970s to hold shareholder meetings on the same day and time (usually the last Thursday in June). The Commercial Code requires that companies closing their books at the end of the fiscal year in April hold a shareholder meeting by the end of June. An increasing number of companies began to cooperate with this policy (which continues today) with the intention of spreading *sokaiya* manpower thin.

Did the Number of Persons Speaking or Raising Questions at a Meeting Change?

The number of persons who speak or raise questions at a shareholder meeting is, according to sources that monitor meeting activity, a euphemistic expression for the number of *sokaiya* disturbing the progress of a meeting. The more persons speaking, the more trouble a company is having, and the less likely the firm paid off potential troublemakers.

There was a definite change in the number of persons speaking out at a meeting in that *sokaiya* were either forced to act alone or in smaller groups. Between 1971 and 1975, an average of 12.08 percent of companies reported between four and six persons raising questions at meetings. This percentage fell from 13.6 percent in 1975 to 5.9 percent in 1976 and averaged 5.51 percent through 1981. Apparently, *sokaiya* were forced to spread their manpower resources to more meetings, given that shareholder meetings were concentrating on a single date.

In sum, increased police activity, coupled with corporate-protection-association actions, seems to have had the following effects:

1. A greater number of firms reporting meetings lasting from one to thirty minutes, and fewer firms reporting meetings lasting longer than thirty minutes.
2. A slight drop among companies reporting no contacts with *sokaiya*, but an increase in the number of companies reporting contacts from a large number of *sokaiya*.
3. More firms reporting no *sokaiya* in attendance at their

meetings, but also a growing number of firms reporting increased *sokaiya* attendance.
4. More firms reporting questions from a smaller number of
sokaiya, with a noticeable drop in the ability of *sokaiya* to
muster manpower for meeting disruptions after 1975, compared to the prior four years.

4

Commercial Code Reform

On June 1, 1973, Takeshi Tanaka, a member of the lower-house Judicial Affairs Committee, held up a batch of newspaper clippings before his colleagues in the Diet.

"Here are two or three days' worth of newspaper articles about the conditions of company-shareholder meetings. I brought these scraps so that we could just take a look at them."

Tanaka read a number of headlines from articles detailing how companies bought off sokaiya *or how* sokaiya *dominated the meetings of firms with applause or speeches and thus prevented other shareholders from raising issues. He singled out Chisso Corporation, which was still locked in a struggle with the Minamata pollution victims. Its shareholder meeting that year lasted all of seven minutes.*

Tanaka then turned to the representative of the Ministry of Justice's Civil Affairs Bureau, asking: "Could you say that this type of activity reflects the intentions of the shareholders?"

The bureaucrat responded in typical fashion:

> *I believe that one could not be satisfied with the condition of shareholder meetings which were described. A properly run shareholder meeting is one where, as much as possible, the operation of the company is discussed and, beyond that, until the*

---

*final decision is made by the shareholders, it is one where criti-
cism should be heard. However, shareholder meetings are concluded in a mere five or ten minutes. Especially, with regard to
this type of meeting, the use of sokaiya is sincerely deplorable
and, I believe, it is only natural that criticism should be raised
against the conditions described. Even though there are various
problems concerning the Commercial Code, at this point the
various committees concerned with the legal system should continue to study the matter. (Kawamoto 1979a, 64)*

This exchange signaled the beginning of what would become
the most thoroughgoing revision of the Japanese Commercial
Code ever conducted. Prior to this reform, there were piece-
meal revisions, important for what they accomplished but
aimed only at a specific problem with one part of the law.
These revisions included reforms in 1911 and 1938 reinforcing the criminal and civil liability of directors, auditors, or
founders of a corporation. These changes reflected those already incorporated into the German model of commercial law,
which was the foundation of the Japanese system. In 1950,
reforms made by the Allied Powers (see chapter 3) attached
an Anglo-American graft to the German model. In 1962 and
1963, accounting methods were improved and strengthened,
as were provisions requiring publication of corporate balance
sheets, profit and loss statements, written management reports,
and related managerial details. In 1966, a stock-transfer system, requiring approval of directors, was enforced. In 1974,
because of a large number of bankruptcies, especially following the end of the Korean War, auditors were given more authority to maintain a watch on the fiscal health of the corporation (Kawamoto et al. 1993, 37–43).

None of these reforms, however, either before or after World
War II, ventured into the conduct of the shareholder meeting

and the problems and issues surrounding it. Abuses of the system were, as Tanaka pointed out, rampant and deplorable.

Debate on Reform Issues

The reform process formally began in July 1973 when the Judicial Affairs Committees of both upper and lower Diet houses backed a study of prospective Commercial Code revisions. Diet debates and questioning of Justice Ministry bureaucrats revealed general agreement that the corporate system needed deep reform. In February 1974, as that year's revision of the Commercial Code passed the Diet, supplementary measures calling for a full-scale revision of the nation's Commercial Code were tacked on the bills and passed through both houses (Kawamoto 1979a, 64–65).

The initial task of outlining the reform package went to the Commercial Code subcommittee of the Legislative Deliberation Commission (Hosei shingikai shohobukai), headed by Takeo Suzuki, professor emeritus at Tokyo University's law school. Such subcommittees develop their own set of legislative proposals, then pass their recommendations to Justice Ministry bureaucrats for a final review before the Diet members are able to vote on the law.

A consultative body of experts such as the Commercial Code subcommittee mentioned above is a normal part of the lawmaking process in Japan. Such groups first appeared in the Japanese lawmaking system during the Allied Occupation, when the Allies attempted to bring more citizen participation into the legislative process. But over the decades, rather than reflecting a wide array of opinions, the membership of these special committees more closely reflected the opinions of the bureaucrats and elite circles who established the committees or served on them.

Participants in the committee were rewarded with recogni-

91

tion of their expertise in the designated field and with the opportunity to achieve higher status by coming into direct contact with other business and intellectual elites, as well as with powerful bureaucrats directly involved in their field of interest. (See Curtis 1975, 33–70, and Passin 1975, 251–83, for detailed discussions of such groups.) Still, given the nature of these groups and this process, the Commercial Code subcommittee's handling of the reform was unusual, at least according to Suzuki, who wrote later: "There was an extremely democratic method employed involving measures approved by the subcommittee being officially approved by the [Justice Ministry's Counselor's Office] and, based on these measures, a wide variety of opinions were sought in order to gather more information" (Suzuki 1981, 22).

Normally, the process of creating or discussing changes in the law took place through deliberations among committee experts and the bureaucrats responsible for that section of the law. In addition, the committee actively sought opinions from groups with a direct interest in the outcome of the legislation through a survey conducted by the Justice Ministry's Civil Affairs Bureau, which is in charge of Commercial Code legislation. The ministry based its questions on the subcommittee's initial findings.

The survey was sent to sixty-one leading members and groups in the academic, legal, and corporate communities in June 1975. They included representatives from the Tokyo High Court and two other high courts (*koto saibansho*), eleven district courts (*chiho saibansho*), Nichibenren (Japan Federation of Bar Associations) and two local bar associations, faculties of law and economics at ten universities, Keidanren (Japan Federation of Economic Organizations) and thirty-five other industry groups, the Japan Certified Public Accountants Association, and the Japan Licensed Tax Accountants Federation (Smith and Tamiya

1978, 102; Inaba 1976, 21–22). (See list at end of chapter.) They represented powerful industrial, commercial, legal, and political interests. Interestingly, not one Minamata protester or antiwar protester was asked to join the discussion.

Reform Survey Issues

The survey covered seven issues, including (listed in order of appearance in the questionnaire): (1) the social responsibility of the corporation; (2) reform of the shareholder-meeting system; (3) reform of the provisions relating to directors and the board of directors; (4) reform of the stock system; (5) corporate accounting and public disclosure; (6) the minimum capital system; and (7) the division of corporations into two categories, namely small and large (Okushima 1981, 39).

The survey asked respondents to provide opinions about each of the seven issues. It also contained short arguments about each issue to aid in answering, but respondents were free to come up with their own ideas.

For the purposes of this study, I am interested only in those sections affecting the social responsibility of the corporation, the shareholder-meeting system, and the stock system. Each issue relates in part to the problem of *sokaiya*–corporate management linkage. At this point, it is helpful to look at the thumbnail arguments presented in the questionnaire, as they reveal what the policymakers were thinking at the time.

On the social responsibility of the corporations:

> Some suggest that a study should be made regarding the feasibility of inserting . . . a general provision dealing with the social responsibility of the corporation, which clearly obligates the directors of corporations to act in ways consistent with social responsibility of their corporations. What is your reaction to this

suggestion? If you find the principle underlying the suggestion acceptable, how would you go about wording such a provision? (Smith and Tamiya 1978, 103)

On reform of the shareholder-meeting system:

There are people who take the view that the general meeting of shareholders has been reduced to a mere ritual or that its operation is less than fair. What improvements do you think should be made (to the meetings) in order to ensure the fair and equitable management of the corporation? (ibid., 104)

On shareholder rights:

Some suggest that the law should specifically provide for the right of the shareholder to ask questions at the shareholders' meeting. What do you think of this? What do you propose in the way of limitations on this right and procedures governing the exercise of the right? (ibid., 105)

On the share system:

Do you feel that it is necessary to change the size of the unit value of shares? Some argue that the minimum value of the unity of par value stock should be raised, while others argue that the system known as the "minimum unit rule" (under which the exercise of the shareholders' right to vote is recognized only when the shareholder holds a certain minimum number of shares) should be adopted. . . . If the minimum unit of stock rule was adopted, do you propose that the rights of those shareholders whose holdings fall short of the minimum amount, including their right to vote, should no longer be recognized? (ibid., 107–8)

On bribery and extortion:

Under the present provisions of Commercial Code Article 494 any person who receives a financial benefit for exercising his voting right so as to accommodate an unlawful solicitation from

> another person is subject to punishment. It has been argued that it should also be an offense for a person to receive an unlawful benefit (a bribe) even in the absence of an unlawful solicitation by another person. . . . What do you think of this? (ibid., 105)

Reports on the answers generated by the questionnaire indicate respondents were wrestling with the theoretical and the practical. How does one balance the theoretical ownership of the corporation by the shareholder with the practical necessities of running a modern corporation?

One commentator, Atsushi Yazawa, a leading academic from Tokyo University, clearly saw the issues as being muddied by their direct link with shareholder rights. However, he was able to draw a line between what he considered the proper use of shareholder rights by directing the corporation's activities in a socially responsible manner and the use of the right to question and make proposals that merely served the political or personal interests of the individual shareholders.

Yazawa was referring to the differences in the actions of American and Japanese one-share stockholder movements. He compared the Beheiren antiwar attacks against Mitsubishi Heavy Industry and the Minamata victims' attacks against Chisso Corporation with the stockholder campaign waged by Ralph Nader against General Motors (which served as the "One-Share Stockholder Movement [OSSM] model). For the Japanese shareholders, Yazawa argued, the protests were not aimed at improving or protecting the welfare of the corporation threatened by management's socially irresponsible actions; rather, the issues were personal or stemmed from their own political or philosophical interests (Yazawa et al. 1975, 22).

His position reflects the opinion, common at the time, that shareholders essentially had only two kinds of rights: the right of common profit and the right of individual profit. The former is, according to one legal scholar of that era, "a right exercised on behalf of the company, involves attending the shareholder meeting, deliberating measures and voting on them. [The latter] is exercised on behalf of the shareholder by, for example, receiving dividends" (Osumi 1971, 9). Both rights are put at risk when corporate action breaks the law or disrupts public order. To protect the rights of common and individual profit from being trampled by such actions, shareholders have a basic responsibility to advise the corporation on how to correct these potentially profit-damaging conditions. However, when shareholders use their rights only to criticize the company, as in the cases of Chisso and Mitsubishi Heavy Industry, companies use this as an excuse to hire protection in the form of *sokaiya* and other private security forces (ibid.).

The use of *sokaiya* as a private-security force from management represented the other extreme contained within the reform debate. This practice was seen by legal reformers as a contributing factor in the ritualization of the shareholder meeting. The meeting would remain nothing more than a shell as long as corporate managers had *sokaiya* to enforce a quick termination of meetings in order to avoid embarrassing questions.

The question was asked: How, then, did one get rid of *sokaiya* without gagging other shareholders? It became a round-robin debate, flowing back into itself at the point of corporate social responsibility, but always extending to shareholder rights as well as corporate ownership and control issues.

Reform Survey Responses

For the survey respondents, opinion was split in a variety of directions. A basic problem was that no one was sure what "corporate social responsibility" actually meant. Further, there were those in the corporate and legal communities who argued that such responsibility either could not be legislated or that it would actually harm the existing commercial law and the corporate organs the law governed.

Respondents from academia, the courts, and medium- and small-enterprise organizations favored inserting provisions to standardize the behavior of corporate directors. Major economic organizations argued that, while provisions could be enacted, they could not easily be enforced. Keidanren, among other large corporate organizations, contended that any talk about supervision of management actions merely catered to the trends of the times and pointed out that no similar provisions existed in any Commercial Code in any other nation. Bar-association representatives and some academics insisted that the issue of management actions be micromanaged within individual systems, including reforming shareholder rights to allow the questioning of corporate officials, requiring detailed explanations of corporate affairs from management, reforming the system to increase and strengthen the powers of outside directors, and placing controls on interlocking directorships among companies (Inaba 1976, 22–23).

From Total to Partial Reform

The Commercial Code subcommittee, survey responses in hand, began deliberating code reformation. It completed the unit-stock-system portion of the reform draft in 1977. A year later, it drafted reforms for corporate-shareholder meetings and other organs. In December 1978, the subcommittee began discussions about accounting practices and public offerings. The reform moved slowly but deliberately through the long list of measures until events outside the subcommittee brought about a drastic change.

Once again, the nation was rocked by a number of corporate problems, the largest being the Lockheed-Grumman scandal, which involved the bribery of Japanese political and government officials in exchange for the awarding of contracts for airplanes. As a result, public outrage against illegal and antisocial corporate actions grew loud (Motoki, Kosugi, and Johnson 1981, 309; Okushima 1981, 41). Suzuki would recall later that pressure from the bureaucracy began to build on him; they wanted to move the process along faster. The pressure was direct.

> In the beginning of the Summer of 1979, at one of the subcommittee meetings, Justice Minister Furui Yoshimi was in attendance and said to me: "There are some who are calling for public authority to be used to supervise corporations in order to prevent more scandals. I am personally completely opposed to this way of thinking and I believe that private companies should use their own internal powers to reduce these incidents. So, as quickly as possible, you should continue with the Commercial Code reform, particularly the supervision and public openness of corporations and think about how to prevent further incidents from taking place."
>
> In reply, I said: "No matter what reform measures we devise, since the public prosecutor doesn't have the authority to investigate (without just cause), I don't think it's possible to expose such scandals."
>
> Furui responded, "Of course, I understand that it's not possible to absolutely prevent these things. However, isn't it better that we at least stop some portion of them?" (Suzuki 1981, 22–23)

In July 1979, shortly after this discussion, the subcommittee agreed to amend its original policy of concentrating on total reform, lowering its sights to partial reforms of those portions of the code governing stock ownership, corporate organs, and accounting and public offerings. The final version of the partial draft reform was submitted to the Minister of Justice's office in January 1981 for further fine-tuning. From there, it moved before the Diet in March 1981 for ratification and received approval in the lower house on May 15, 1981, and in the upper house on June 3, 1981 (Okushima and Nose 1982, 89; Okushima and Yamada 1983, 121).

The reform package contained eight sections, but only two directly affected conditions relating to *sokaiya*: the enforcement of the Minimum Unit Stock Rule and a tightening of laws against solicitations or offers of bribes in exchange for exercising shareholder rights (either to use those rights to ask questions or not use those rights by not asking questions).

Minimum Unit Stock Rule

The Minimum Unit Stock Rule requires a person to own shares worth fifty thousand yen in a corporation before that individual is eligible to exercise shareholder voting rights and privileges at shareholder meetings. Those with fewer than the minimum units would still retain the right to dividends and other attendant rights as prescribed by the Commercial Code (Okushima and Nose 1982, 90–91).

Mark E. Foster, a legal scholar, predicted that the use of the rule would likely eliminate small-lot shareholders from participating in the corporate system, because the common par value of shares prior to code reform was fifty yen, compared to fifty thousand yen after code reform. However, he notes that the stock exchanges were already establishing a minimum level of one thousand shares per transaction for fifty-yen par-value stock, "thereby already having effectively instituted a 50,000 yen minimum trading unit." Further, since those without a minimum share unit had no right to speak at shareholder meetings, it was believed that this would eliminate a major portion of *sokaiya* who would find it too costly to attend and disrupt meetings (Foster 1983, 588–89). And yet the same could be said about members of the OSSM. If this portion eliminated some *sokaiya* from meetings, it effectively decapitated the OSSM strategy as an effective form of mass protest.

Prohibitions Against Bribery

The second important reform was the broadening of existing provisions against the use of *sokaiya*. Under the revised Article 494:

> Persons who have, in response to unlawful solicitations, received, demanded or entered into an agreement to receive or to give any benefit of a proprietary nature . . . shall be liable to imprisonment with hard labor for a term not exceeding one year or to a fine not exceeding five hundred thousand yen. (EHS 1991, 162)

Article 494 covered actions by *sokaiya* such as making a statement or exercising a right to vote at a shareholder meeting or exercising other rights of a shareholder.

A second provision, Article 497, stated:

> If a director, auditor, acting director or manager or other employee has, for account of the company, offered any benefit of a proprietary nature in relation to exercise of the right of a shareholder, he shall be liable to penal servitude not exceeding six months, or a fine not exceeding three hundred thousand yen. (ibid., 163)

Thus both *sokaiya* and corporate officers and employees were not made equally responsible for "unlawful solicitations."

But these provisions covered only the use of corporate funds to buy the use of shareholder rights, and made those involved in such activities liable to the corporation and subject to criminal charges. Personal funds, however, could still be used. As such, "an incumbent director may bestow benefits on other shareholders out of his pocket with the purpose of securing their votes for his re-election" (Motoki, Kosugi, and Johnson 1981, 331). Similarly, there were no provisions against making gratuitous payments to people who were not shareholders of the corporation at the time they received the payment (Foster 1983, 599).

Obviously, then, managers could easily outwit the legal reforms by using their own money or by paying a *sokaiya* prior to his purchase of any of that corporation's stock. One source involved in dealing with *sokaiya* at the time recalls all employees in the general affairs department of a corporation suddenly receiving double and triple their regular summer and winter bonuses—a typical bonus amounting to several months of an employee's salary. The employees then were informed that the money would be funneled back to the department head, who would use it for payoffs to *sokaiya*. On the corporation's books, however, the money was hidden as a salary payment to employees. Clearly, the system had not really changed at all.

Shifting Debate

The debates among survey respondents and others concerned with Commercial Code reform shifted dramatically in just a few years from rather esoteric discussions about shareholder rights and the social responsibility of the corporation to the practicalities of shareholder-meeting reform and elimination of *sokaiya*.

This shift was at least partly due to the personal intervention of Justice Minister Furui, who was himself pressured by the corporate scandals of the mid-1970s. Even today, it is difficult to determine what other motivating factors pushed Furui to intervene. He was a political appointee from the Liberal Democratic

Party (LDP)—a party that was and still is deeply involved with and beholden to big business interests. Moreover, at that time, LDP members were direct beneficiaries of Lockheed-Grumman payoffs. Hence, action of some sort would relieve pressure on the party to take more drastic, antibusiness action. It would weaken arguments or charges raised by opposition parties.

In sum, although the reform debate initially considered the OSSM strategy of mass anticorporate protests, by the late 1970s the focus was on *sokaiya*. In effect, the establishment of the minimum-share-unit rule and tightened restrictions on corporate payouts in return for exercising shareholder rights were both intended, at least partially, to be anti-*sokaiya* countermeasure provisions.

The question, then, is: Did the reform have the intended consequences of cutting ties between *sokaiya* and corporations?

List of Organizations Responding to Questionnaire

Legal Entities

District Courts (Chiho Saibansho)
First Tokyo Bar Association (Dai-Ichi Tokyo Bengoshikai)
Japan Federation of Bar Associations (Nihon Bengoshi Rengokai)
Kobe Bar Association (Kobe Bengoshikai)
Supreme Court (Koto Saibansho)

Academic Entities

Ajia University Commercial Code Research Group (Ajia Daigaku Shoho Kenkyukai)
Hitotsubashi Daigaku Hogakubu
Keio University Commercial Code Research Group (Keio Daigaku Shoho Kenkyukai)

Kobe Shoka Daigaku, Shokei Gakubu, Shoho-Kaikeigaku Kenkyukai
Kyoto Sangyo Daigaku (Professor Sato)
Kyushu Daigaku Shoho Kenkyukai
Nagoya University Law Faculty (Nagoya Daigaku Hogakubu)
Senshu Daigaku Hogakubu
Waseda Daigaku Hogakubu

Economic Groups

Chiba-ken Chusho Kigyo Dantai Chuokai (Chiba Small and Medium Business Federation)
Denki Jigyo Rengokai (Federation of Electric Power Companies)
Fukuoka Shoko Kaigisho (Fukuoka Chamber of Commerce and Industry)
Hyogo-ken Chusho Kigyo Dantai Chuokai (Hyogo Small and Medium Business Federation)
Ita Garasu Kyokai (Flat Glass Association of Japan)
Kagawa-ken Chusho Kigyo Dantai Chuokai (Hyogo Small and Medium Business Federation)
Kanagawa-ken Chusho Kigyo Dantai Chuokai (Kanagawa Small and Medium Business Federation)
Kansai Keizai Rengokai (Kansai Economic Federation)
Keizai Dantai Rengokai (Federation of Economic Organizations)
Kobe Shoko Kaigisho (Kobe Chamber of Commerce and Industry)
Koshasai Hikiuke Kyokai (Bond Underwriters Association of Japan)
Kyoto Shoko Kaigisho (Kyoto Chamber of Commerce and Industry)
Nagoya Shoko Kaigisho (Nagoya Chamber of Commerce and Industry)
Nihon Gomu Kogyokai (Japan Rubber Manufacturers Association)
Nihon Insatsu Kogyokai (Japan Printers Association)
Nihon Shinbun Kyokai (The Japan Newspaper Publishers and Editors Association)
Nihon Tekko Renmei (Japan Iron and Steel Federation)
Nippon Boekikai (Japan Foreign Trade Council, Inc.)
Nippon Denki Kogyokai (Japan Electrical Manufacturers' Association)
Nippon Jidosha Kogyokai (Japan Automobile Manufacturers Association)
Nippon Minei Tetsudo Kyokai (Japan Non-Government Railways Association)
Nippon Seishi Rengokai (Japan Paper Association)
Nippon Shokengyo Kyokai (Securities Dealers Association of Japan)
Nippon Songai Hoken Kyokai (Marine and Fire Insurance Association of Japan)

Nippon Zosen Kogyokai (Shipbuilders' Association of Japan)
Osaka Kogyokai (Osaka Industrial Association)
Osaka Shoko Kaigisho (Osaka Chamber of Commerce and Industry)
Sekiyu Renmei Zaimu Iinkai (Petroleum Association of Japan, Financial Affairs Committee)
Shintaku Kyokai (Trust Companies' Association of Japan)
Sogo Ginko Kyokai (Association of Sogo Banks)
Tokyo Shoken Torihikijo (Tokyo Stock Exchange)
Tokyo Shoko Kaigisho (Tokyo Chamber of Commerce and Industry)
Zenkoku Chusho Kigyo Dantai Chuokai (National Federation of Small Business Associations)
Zenkoku Ginko Kyokai Rengokai (Federation of Bankers' Associations of Japan)
Zenkoku Shokokai Rengokai (Central Federation of Societies of Commerce and Industry, Japan)

Other Concerned Groups

Daiichi Zeirishi Kyogikai (First Council of Certified Public Tax Accountants)
Kinyu Zaisei Jijo Kenkyukai (Institute for Financial Affairs, Inc.)
Nagoya Kabushiki Jinmu Kenkyukai
Nihon Kansayaku Kyokai
Nihon Konin Kaikeishi Kyokai (Japan Institute of Certified Public Accountants)
Nihon Konin Kaikeishi Kyokai Kinki-kai (Japan Institute of Certified Public Accountants, Kinki Group)
Nihon Shiho Shoshikai Rengokai
Nihon Zeirishikai Rengokai (Japan Federation of Certified Public Tax Accountants Association)
Osaka Kabushiki Jimmu Kondankai
Shoji Homu Kenkyukai–Keiei Hoyukai
Tokyo Kabushiki Konwakai

5

Sokaiya Maintain Position

In April 1991, some seventy sokaiya *and corporate executives of the general affairs departments of major Japanese corporations met at Chiyoda, a* ryotei *(high-class Japanese restaurant) in Tokyo.[1] Mitsuyoshi Miharu, a prominent* sokaiya *in the Tokyo area, was the host.*

According to restaurant workers interviewed by Asahi Shimbun, *the banquet probably cost 50,000 yen per person, totaling 3.5 million yen. The party activities included a lottery, with the first prize being a trip to Europe and the second prize a trip to the United States. The costs of the "trips" brought the estimated total of the affair to some 5 million yen, or about $50,000, and only corporate executives in attendance could win the lottery. However, winners did not receive airline tickets and hotel-reservation chits. Instead, they were handed envelopes containing cash in amounts meant to cover the cost of the trips. Obviously, the envelopes contained payoffs—the twist being that they came from a* sokaiya *to corporate managers, rather than the other way around.*

The managers later told reporters that each had received a personal telephone call from Miharu requesting their presence at the party. Among the oldest attendees was a seventy-five-year-old representative from Mitsubishi Materials Corporation who had been working as an intermediary with sokaiya *for four decades. The man's assistant explained: "All he said to me was that there was this get-together and that he seemed to feel that it was his responsibility to show up and be seen among all the other* sokaiya *managers."*

Other managers in attendance later expressed concern and even regret about agreeing to attend: "I thought something would happen afterward. Just what, I couldn't tell. Would something be said? Would someone be arrested? I didn't know. If I think about it now, I guess it was Miharu who paid for the whole thing. I guess he could use that against us when he makes a demand of us."

Another guest said, "I think it was purely a demonstration of Miharu's power and that was the sole intention—to show off how important he is." Still another said, "I've been dealing with Miharu for more than ten years; before the Corporate Code reform. But considering the numbers of people present, the fact that there was a lottery, and the spirit and closeness of association between sokaiya *and managers which was demonstrated in the room, I rather lightly made the decision to go. Now I figure I was a bit rash in doing it."*

As the above incident illustrates, nearly a decade after reform, *sokaiya* and corporation managers still maintained a close association. Although the legal reform of the Commercial Code should have prevented *sokaiya* from maintaining their influence and power over corporate executives, Miharu clearly proved that such was not the case. Why was this so?

In his analysis of the adaptation of the Sicilian Mafia to changes in political, legal, and economic conditions in Italy, Raimondo Catanzaro seems to be describing the situation in Japan as well, especially as it relates to *sokaiya*:

> [T]he continuity of the mafia derives from its capacity to adapt continually to change. This happens because the mafia groups are not relics of the past, but were formed as a result of a specific combination of ancient and modern, a mixture of private violence and legitimate violence of the state, of competition for economic resources in the market and the absence of regulatory standards for economic activities other than violence. (Catanzaro 1985, 34)

While it would be unrealistic to equate *sokaiya* with the huge and multifaceted organizations forming the Mafia, *sokaiya* nevertheless also have been able to maintain their position within the Japanese corporate system for many of the same reasons cited by Catanzaro. By using violence or the threat of violence on behalf of or against corporate managers as a way of achieving economic and social status, *sokaiya* embedded themselves in the system throughout the twentieth century.

The 1982 Commercial Code reform was intended to regulate the entry of *sokaiya* into the shareholder-meeting system. In effect, it was supposed to force managers to end their reliance on *sokaiya* by tightening restrictions on payoffs that would buy shareholder rights. Just prior to reform, some *sokaiya* took extreme measures to ensure their place in the system would be protected.

The April 16, 1981, edition of the *Wall Street Journal* ran an unusual story on the front page. The headline tagged the story as a "quirky" feature, designed to relieve some of the gray heaviness of the newspaper's more serious financial and news stories: "Japan Exports Way to Quiet Stockholders."

Journalists Rustin and Kanabayashi reported in the story that one of the largest known *sokaiya* organizations, Rondan Doyukai (described in chapter 1), spent some $232,000 for shareholder rights in twelve American and three European corporations listed on the Tokyo Stock Exchange. The firms included General Motors, BankAmerica, Atlantic Richfield, American Express, Chase Manhattan, Citicorp, First Chicago, International Business Machines, IU International, Sperry, Dow Chemical, International Telephone and Telegraph, Rotterdamsch Beleggingsconsortium, Compagnie Française des Pétroles, and Compagnie Financière de Paris et des Pays-Bas.

In an interview with the reporters, Rondan chief Masayuki Kajitani said his organization was not a *sokaiya* group, as had been charged, but rather a "check organization for the sound operation of enterprises. So sometimes we behave as lawyers, sometimes as prosecutors and sometimes as journalists." He said that overseas his group would be better able to learn how shareholder-meeting practices differ from those in Japan and how Japanese shareholders could exercise their rights as foreign stockholders.

Given what we already know about *sokaiya*, it would be appropriate to think that they were trying to get payoffs from foreign firms. But that was not the case. Instead, they began to contact the home offices of the foreign corporations in pursuit of information on Japanese companies with ties to the foreign firms. For example, BankAmerica's shareholder meeting was held on April 21, 1981. The proceedings were reported on page 4 of the next day's *Wall Street Journal* and included this paragraph:

> The lengthiest questions at the meeting came from several Japanese holders, whom a bank official identified as members of a *sokaiya* group . . . They pressed bank officials for details of loans to a Japanese company. The bank declined to comment, citing confidentiality. (O'Donnell 1981, 4)

The following year, with reform measures now in place, the group was intimately involved with the downfall of the president of Mitsukoshi Department Store who was found to be embezzling funds from the company in order to support his mistress, her boutique, and their affair. Rondan formed the "Mitsukoshi Mamoru-kai," or "Protect Mitsukoshi Group," which used shareholder meetings to campaign for the president's resignation. The resignation was an outstanding display of power for the group and affected the company long after. By 1988, the *Japan Company Handbook*, a comprehensive listing of all companies on the Tokyo Stock Exchange, reported the following about Mitsukoshi: "Time-honored department store long serving as leader of Mitsui group . . . bounding back from sales setback and marred image caused by misbehaved ex-president" (*Japan Company Handbook* 1988, 909).

In spite of the display of power by Rondan and other *sokaiya*—some managed to stall the 1984 Sony meeting for thirteen and a half hours—did the legal reform have its intended effect? Did the number of *sokaiya* fall and taper off? Did Japanese shareholder meetings grow longer as "legitimate" shareholders exercised their rights without fear of verbal or physical abuse? Did nearly a decade of debate fundamentally alter the view that *sokaiya* were a "necessary evil"?

The increasing number of gangsters entering the *sokaiya* milieu revealed that surface activities by police and corporate managers had actually little effect on *sokaiya*. More, not fewer *sokaiya* became active, in spite of the establishment of protective associations designed to allow corporations to cut their ties to *sokaiya*. The threat of mass demonstrations that existed in the early 1970s was long gone, and yet *sokaiya* found their occupation even more lucrative than before. They adapted to changing conditions. But what about legal reform? Did the 1982 Commercial Code reform have the intended effect of breaking the links between corporations and gangsters?

Paper Changes

On the surface, the number of *sokaiya* known by the police to be active and reported in its annual white papers dropped dramatically in the years after reform took effect. In 1982, just prior to reform, the *sokaiya* population was estimated by the National Police Agency (NPA) at approximately 6;800; it plummeted to 1,700 after reform, and has settled to between 1,200 and 1,300 since then (National Police Agency 1982, 122–23). However, the drop was not caused solely by tighter restrictions on payoffs and increased prosecutions—a common belief among many observers (*Mainichi shimbun* 1994, 5). Rather, the drop in the *sokaiya* population was a "paper change" brought about by the modification in what constitutes a shareholder with rights in Japan.

According to the amended code, a person is required to own at least one thousand shares of a corporation's stock before gaining the right to ask questions, make motions, and vote at shareholder meetings. Prior to reform, an active *sokaiya* could own just a few shares and exercise such rights. The reform thus essentially legislated out of existence a number of *sokaiya* who, because they did not hold a sufficient number of shares, did not qualify as regular shareholders—but by no means did they disappear from the scene. And yet this point is never revealed in the NPA white papers published in the years following reform. Instead, the implication is that reform had dealt a smashing blow to *sokaiya* themselves, slashing the entire population by an incredible 75 percent. One police official explained with embarrassment, "We are a success, but only on paper."

In private police publications that the public seldom if ever sees, the effect of Commercial Code reform is more clearly represented and somewhat different.[2] As mentioned above, the annual NPA white paper reported a *sokaiya* population of 6,800 in 1982. The following year, that active population fell to 1,682. Technically, this corresponds with the private police document estimate of about 1,700 *sokaiya* in 1983. However, the private publication also notes an additional 2,300 persons who, while not technically defined as *sokaiya* based on the Commercial Code–reform criteria for acquisition of shareholder rights, still operate within *sokaiya* extortion rackets. These individuals are described as "newspaper ruffians" (*shinbun goro*), "company ruffians" (*kaisha goro*), and "others" (*sono ta*) (Violent Group Countermeasures [VGC], 1994, 9–10, 28). Similar to regular *sokaiya* who work within the shareholder-meeting structure, these individuals commit extortion, either by publishing embarrassing newspaper articles about corporate executives' private lives or mistakes made in the operation of the corporations, or through direct threats or other disturbances (see chapter 1).

In reality, then, the police-reported 75 percent drop in the *sokaiya* population is actually closer to 40 percent—in other words, nearly 60 percent of the pre-reform *sokaiya* population remained intact following the code reforms designed to eliminate them. Hence despite reform efforts, *sokaiya* were able to maintain their positions through ownership of the required number of shares, or they continued their work through other traditional methods, such as publication of small tabloids carrying scandalous articles about targeted companies. Nevertheless, even a 40 percent drop in the *sokaiya* population has to be considered significant, which leads to the question, What happened to the other *sokaiya*—those neither active in shareholder meetings nor involved in secondary forms of extortion?

Sokaiya Adaptation

Some *sokaiya* continued to extort corporations, but now under the guise of right-wing political groups. Such groups generally are labeled by police and observers as "right-wing *sokaiya*" (*uyoku sokaiya*) or "pseudo right-wing groups" (*ese uyoku dantai*). Tactically, this strategy is a potentially safer and more rewarding method of extortion for a number of reasons.

First, pseudo right-wing groups receive immediate protection under constitutional guarantees of equal treatment under the law (Article 14), freedom of thought (Article 19), and freedom of association and expression (Article 21) (Keibi jitsumu kenkyukai-cho [KJK] 1989, 154). Thus, under the guise of political activity, they are able to mask their harassment while gaining some measure of constitutional protection that is obviously unavailable to mainstream *sokaiya*. (However, most traditional *sokaiya* refuse to employ such tactics, as these so-called political groups are often derided as "fakes" unable to succeed as "true" *sokaiya*.)

Second, *sokaiya* who adopt right-wing personae allow themselves a wider range of available activities and potential for profit. No longer limited solely to the yearly shareholder meetings, they are able to mount campaigns against a corporation or its managers whenever the opportunity arises—even if that opportunity must be manufactured.

Such campaigns are fairly simple in form and execution. Most rightist groups in Japan use large vehicles, such as buses and trucks, painted in gray, black, or sometimes camouflage, and most are equipped with loudspeakers. The windows are heavily screened, presumably in anticipation of attack. The vehicles are usually parked outside major train stations or areas where large numbers of potential listeners congregate. Often the group's leader or its most eloquent speaker will climb atop the vehicle, flanked by several intimidating bodyguards, and speak on some issue of importance to the group and/or the right wing in general (e.g., reverence for the emperor, return of territories held by Russia since the end of World War II, or complaints about corrupt politicians and the harm they cause common citizens). The vehicles also are useful in harassment campaigns against corporations or executives. In such cases, they are parked outside company headquarters or driven through neighborhoods where executives reside. While martial music blares, a speech is delivered enumerating the alleged misdeeds of the target. Often, money is incentive enough to send these groups on their way.

There are many examples of right-wing groups employed by the Liberal Democratic Party (LDP) and corporations to help suppress groups or individuals who threatened the postwar status quo. Used as police reinforcements, such groups helped to suppress labor unions during the bloody 1960 conflict over the U.S.–Japan Security Treaty; as street fighters, they physically subdued the Beheiren and Minamata protesters. In each case they acted at the request of corporate managers or political elites. More recently, a pseudo right-wing group known as Nippon Komin-to (Japan Emperor and People Party) with ties to the Yamaguchi-gumi crime syndicate engaged in a *homegoroshi* (killing-with-praise) campaign against Noboru Takeshita, who would eventually become prime minister.[3]

Killing with Praise

Nippon Komin-to was founded in 1972 by the Yamaguchi-gumi subgroup Shiragame-gumi, led at that time by Toruo Inamoto. Inamoto had been asked to form the group by Hideo Shiragame, himself a high-level member of Yamaguchi-gumi who was involved in *sokaiya* activities as well as right-wing operations at various times during the 1970s. It is not clear who hired the group to conduct its campaign against Takeshita; however, the campaign began in early 1987, shortly after Takeshita bolted from the political faction of longtime LDP kingpin, Kakue Tanaka. Nippon Komin-to drove its sound trucks through the streets of Tokyo around the Diet building and national government-office district, announcing their support for Takeshita and his bid for LDP party presidency and, automatically at that time, the premiership. Their general message was: "Takeshita *Sensei* [teacher] is the best choice for prime minister because he is so capable of getting money from others."

The campaign was an embarrassment to Takeshita, who at the time was attempting to build his own faction. Few politicians would be desirous of joining forces with him if they, too, would consequently become right-wing targets. The campaign ended only after the intercession of other party leaders, businessmen, and several top members of crime syndicates. Large sums of money were offered to Nippon Komin-to leaders to end the campaign, but, according to insiders, the money was rejected, perhaps because of the long-standing feud between Takeshita and Yamaguchi-gumi leaders. The feud began in the early 1980s, when Takeshita was finance minister and had to decide which banking or management group would assume control of the failing Heiwa Sogo Bank. Sumitomo Bank wanted it for itself, because in acquiring Heiwa Sogo, Sumitomo would become the largest financial institution in the Tokyo region. Yamaguchi-gumi leaders, on the other hand, already had a relationship with Heiwa Sogo, and hoped that a member of its board would take over the bank and thus provide Japan's largest crime syndicate with its own friendly financial institution. We will probably never really know what the real reason or reasons were for the refusal of money by Komin-to leaders. Instead of cash, they demanded that Takeshita publicly apologize to Tanaka for deserting the faction when Tanaka's health was failing and political lights were growing dim. The affair was eventually settled by the intercession of Susumu Ishii, who at the time was head of the powerful Tokyo-based syndicate, Inagawa-kai. Takeshita never apologized publicly, but it is not clear even today what was done to end the campaign.

Mundane Affairs

On occasion, right-wing *sokaiya* involvement in elite affairs is more mundane, yet still falls in the realm of *sokaiya* performing mercenary services in disputes. For example, according to a private police report, the chairman of an electrical appliance company planned the forced retirement of the firm's president, employing gangsters and right-wing *sokaiya* to execute the coup. On April 17, 1990, the president was at the construction site of a company sales center when a number of gangsters and right-wing *sokaiya* appeared and attempted to intimidate him into resigning. The president did not contact police until some years later, and arrests were made on March 3, 1993, three years after the initial event. Although the outcome of the arrests is not known, it is important to note that those involved in intracorporate disputes have a ready resource (*sokaiya*) available to them and clearly understand how to make use of that resource (Violent Group Countermeasures [VGC] 1994, 15–16).

As one observer noted:

> Companies who have problems are weak. The right-wing groups write in their organization publications about internal and external quarrels, or make repeated calls to homes and all of this can be put in order by money. Afterwards they trail their target around, suggesting a get-together. Ultimately executives don't bear all of the responsibility for this situation. The police, too, are weak in the face of the right-wing groups. So, except in extreme cases, corporate executives don't report incidents. (Takagi 1989, 70)

Besides using the cover of right-wing political parties, some *sokaiya* groups began to hide behind the front of *burakumin* civil-rights organizations to run extortion campaigns. *Burakumin*, or social outcasts, suffer ongoing discrimination at all levels of mainstream Japanese society. Extortion groups use the ideology of the *burakumin* movement to squeeze payoffs and contributions from companies wanting to avoid public criticism for discriminatory practices. Some three hundred extortion groups are known to operate in Japan using the *burakumin* cover. In actuality, only four organizations inside the liberation movement—Zen Nihon Dowa-kai, Buraku Kaiho Domei, Zen Nihon Buraku Kaiho Undo Rengokai, and Zen Nihon Jiyu Dowa-kai—are considered legitimate civil-rights organizations seeking redress for past and continuing discrimination practices (Kawauchi 1993, 263–5).

Right-Wing *Sokaiya* Income

For such groups as these, "donations" from companies are a main source of income, and because such payments can be made as political contributions without connection to shareholder meetings, they avoid the Commercial Code provisions against payoffs to shareholders. In one study of right-wing finances conducted in the early 1980s, donations comprised between 34 and 43 percent of the average group's income. Group work accounted for another 21 to 38 percent, and the remainder was raised through party and group dues. The majority of donations and support funding came from companies. In contrast, left-wing groups reported about one-quarter of their income coming from donations, with 40 percent coming from private individuals. The dependence of right-wing groups on corporations is clear (Takagi 1989, 68).

In sum, while the Commercial Code reform of 1982 had some effect on the overall *sokaiya* population, it was largely on paper. Those racketeers eliminated from the shareholder-meeting process because they did not have enough shares engaged in other forms of mainstream *sokaiya* activity or took on right-wing personae to continue in their trade. Clearly, the argument that the reform actually curbed *sokaiya* activity is weak.

Reform Effects on Meetings

Even with the adaptation of some *sokaiya* to the changed conditions under legal reform, did the reform substantively change the conditions of shareholder meetings? An examination of statistics gathered by the legal journal *Shoji homu* on the operation of shareholder meetings from 1982 through 1993 indicates that some changes took place following code reform. The years reform took place are not entirely representative of the years prior to or following enforcement of the measures. Statistics might be skewed by implementation of the reform package.

However, when compared with shareholder-meeting statistics published in the years prior to code reform (reviewed previously), the changes after 1982 are indeed great. As in the previous examination of these statistics (see chapter 4), they must be considered with the same cautions: they may reflect the "face" some companies hope to present to the *Shoji homu* researchers. They may be altered so that attention is not drawn to their firm. Executives may not admit to meeting with *sokaiya* or having any trouble with *sokaiya* at all. And there is the problem of how to identify *sokaiya* from among all shareholders. This new problem arose when, after 1982, contacts with *sokaiya* were now termed contacts with *kodo ma-ku kabunushi* or "shareholders marked active." The new designation is apparently a reaction to the law prohibiting contact with *sokaiya*.

Did Meeting Length Change After Reform?

The traditional indicator of antimanagement *sokaiya* presence at meetings is the length of time needed to run the meeting. Short meetings usually indicate that company managers have made payoffs to troublesome *sokaiya* or have arranged for protection with one or more *sokaiya* groups to suppress others.

From 1971 through 1981, the vast majority of meetings (91.4 percent) lasted on average thirty minutes or less. Only 0.6 percent of meetings lasted more than one hour. Following the 1982 reform, there was a sharp drop, to 56.5 percent, in meetings lasting less than thirty minutes. However, after 1983, shareholder meetings lasting less than thirty minutes gradually increased. Although never to the levels prior to code reform, by 1993, 80 percent of shareholder meetings lasted less than thirty minutes. In other words, over time, the effect of reform dropped off.

At the same time, there was also a significant boost in the number of meetings lasting between thirty minutes and an hour, but this number also fell off over time. Moreover, there was an appreciable increase in the number of meetings lasting more than an hour, and even though this number eventually fell, it is far higher in 1993 (4.3 percent) than in the years 1971 through 1981 (0.6 percent). However, before any conclusions can be drawn from this data, the effect of code reform in other categories should be examined.

What Was the Effect of the Minimum-Unit Rule?

The minimum-unit rule required any person wishing to exercise shareholder rights to own a minimum number of shares before they could exercise shareholder rights (see chapter 4).

This rule did seem to have an effect. Most companies reported no *sokaiya* at their meetings from 1983 onward (42 percent in 1983, increasing to 68.8 percent by 1993), probably because the meetings took place on the last Thursday in June and because of the loss of shareholder rights among some *sokaiya*. Fewer *sokaiya* attended fewer company shareholder meetings all held on the same day. This would also be partly due to the fact that some *sokaiya* were legislated out of the process. However, more than 10 percent of firms still report *sokaiya* in their midst. Clearly, money still could be made by attending meetings, although not on the level nor to the extent of the years prior to reform when nearly the opposite was reported (12.4 percent of companies claimed no *sokaiya* attended their meetings between 1975 and 1981).

Did Shareholder Participation Change?

After reform, the meetings became quieter, with little or no participation by shareholders beyond casting their votes. From 1971 through 1981, an average of 20.56 percent of company managers heard no comments from those attending meetings. From 1983 onward, the number of meetings without any questions or comments from attendees hovered at approximately 85 percent, on average. A single speaker was heard at about 7 percent, while by the late 1980s about 10 percent of shareholder meetings had between one and three speakers.

Did Sokaiya *Contacts with Companies Lessen?*

Given that meetings were running only slightly longer after reform than before, that the number of *sokaiya* in attendance at meetings declined, and that the number of relatively quiet shareholder meetings grew, one might conclude that *sokaiya* either were forced further underground or that payoff money flowed faster and more plentifully from corporations.

The data suggest that *sokaiya* became more active after reform and used their manpower resources more efficiently. From 1975 through 1981, an average of only 2.5 percent of Japanese corporations claimed no contacts with *sokaiya*. Some 13.9 percent reported contacts with between one and fifty *sokaiya*, and 17.8 percent reported contacts with between fifty-one and a hundred *sokaiya*. More than one-third of all Japanese companies in the survey reported that they dealt with between 101 and three hundred *sokaiya*, while nearly 20 percent claimed contacts with 301 or more. Some 9.6 percent of firms refused to answer the question.

After Commercial Code reform, the number of firms reporting no contact increased, growing from 3.1 percent in 1983 to 17.2 percent by 1993; those reporting contacts with fifty-one or more *sokaiya* dropped precipitously to about 2 percent overall by 1993. However, the number of companies reporting contacts with between one and fifty *sokaiya* exploded to about 80 percent by the late 1980s. Clearly, although fewer *sokaiya* were active at meetings, they were indeed more active in making contacts with company officials.

Did the Minimum-Unit Rule Have an Effect?

Respondents to *Shoji homu*'s surveys for 1981 through 1983 were asked whether the minimum-unit rule would have an effect on the number of *sokaiya* attending meetings. In 1981, 67 percent of respondents were generally positive that the rule would cause some reduction, while an additional 23 percent thought they would see a major reduction. By 1982, opinion was shifting, split evenly with 47 percent seeing a major reduction and 47 percent seeing some reduction. In 1983, the mood shifted to an even more positive note, with 57.3 percent saying the rule would cause a major reduction in the number of *sokaiya* at meetings. Another 39.2 percent believed some reduction would take place. The remainder spread between "no effect," "opposite effect," and no response.

Will Code Reform Be Effective?

Managers were also asked if they viewed the law prohibiting payoffs for the exercise of shareholder rights as an effective countermeasure to *sokaiya* demands. In 1981, some 36 percent thought the new legislation would be very helpful, while 50.6 percent believed it would be somewhat helpful, and 8.9 percent answered that reform would not help. By 1983, pessimism was largely gone, with only 1.1 percent saying it would not help, 11.2 percent responding it would be somewhat helpful, and 85.6 percent responding reform would be very helpful.

Accordingly, a large number of Japanese corporate managers believed they would be able to achieve through legal reform what they could not accomplish through years of payoffs—the accomplishment being short meetings relatively undisturbed by questions or comments from shareholders, particularly unfriendly *sokaiya*. Moreover, armed with the new rule prohibiting payment to *sokaiya* to remain silent at meetings, management could turn away those *sokaiya* they considered weak. It is important to note, however, that the main goal of the reformers—to eliminate the link between corporate managers and *sokaiya*—was not met. Arguably, the link was weakened but never severed.

Post-Reform Scandals

As shown earlier in this chapter, *sokaiya* remain embedded in the Japanese corporate system in spite of reforms designed to eliminate them.

Sokaiya used a variety of methods to adapt their extortion rackets to changed conditions. Corporate meetings are not necessarily their sole means of income. If they are powerful enough, they can receive payoffs in the form of goodwill payments at parties or by acting as real-estate brokers and small-time newspaper or newsletter publishers. Moreover, since corporate managers fear revelations of scandal or misdeeds either by themselves or other personnel, *sokaiya* can use that fear to kill rumors or spread them. In either case, payoffs are necessary, and this, apparently, is fundamentally why *sokaiya* can continue to profit in their operations for or against Japanese corporations. Perhaps this can be made more clear upon examination of a number of incidents where *sokaiya* and corporate managers were found in collusion, arrested, charged, and tried in the years following the 1982 reform.

More than twenty incidents involving arrests of corporate managers and *sokaiya* were found in violation of Commercial Code Articles 494 and 497 prohibiting payoffs for the exercise of shareholder rights ("Kabunushi sokai gaikyo—Ichigatsu sokai" 1993, 84–85). A partial review may show how conditions have not changed in spite of code reform.

Osaka Henatsuki. A company section chief and seven *sokaiya* were arrested by Osaka police in October 1984 for payoffs totaling 990,000 yen. The section chief was sentenced to five months' imprisonment, suspended for two years. The *sokaiya* were sentenced to an average two years' imprisonment, suspended for three years.

Sogo. The head of the secretary's office and three *sokaiya* were arrested by Osaka police in July 1986 for payoffs amounting to 150,000 yen. The executive was fined 150,000 yen and the *sokaiya* were fined 100,000 yen each.

Noritake. Three executives and four *sokaiya* from four separate groups were arrested by Aiichi prefecture police in July 1986 for payoffs totaling 8.45 million yen. The executives were sentenced to six months' imprisonment, suspended for four years. The *sokaiya* were sentenced to five months' imprisonment.

Sumitomo Marine and Fire Insurance. Two members of the general affairs department and one *sokaiya* were arrested in April 1987 by the NPA for payoffs totaling two million yen. The executives were sentenced to two months' imprisonment, suspended. The *sokaiya* was sentenced to six months' imprisonment, suspended for three years.

Kyowa Dengyo (Kyowa Electronic Instruments). Three members of the general affairs department and two *sokaiya* were arrested in February 1988 by the NPA for payoffs involving 4 million yen. The executives received an average sentence of six months' imprisonment, suspended for three years. The *sokaiya* were sentenced to an average six months' imprisonment, suspended for four years.

Parco. A former managing director, two employees, and two *sokaiya* were arrested in October 1988 by the NPA for payoffs totaling 2 million yen. The executives were sentenced to an average five months' imprisonment, suspended for two years. The *sokaiya* were sentenced to five months' imprisonment, suspended.

Fuji Fire and Marine Insurance. A director, two other employees, and four *sokaiya* were arrested in May 1989 by the Osaka police for payoffs involving 2 million yen. The executives were sentenced to an average five months' imprisonment, suspended for two years. The *sokaiya* were sentenced to an average eighteen months' imprisonment, suspended for three years.

Heiwado. An executive director, six employees, and one *sokaiya* were arrested by Kyoto police in April 1991 for payoffs totaling 700,000 yen. One executive was fined 150,000 yen.

Nikko Securities, Yamaichi Securities, Nomura Securities, and Daiwa Securities. Seven executives were arrested in total: at Nikko, the general affairs department vice chief and the chief of the general affairs stock section; at Yamaichi, the general affairs department external chief; at Nomura, the external department chief of the secretary's office and a former director of the same office; at Daiwa, the former general affairs chief and the chief of the general affairs department. Two *sokaiya* were arrested. All arrests took place in June 1991 for payoffs totaling 3.5 million yen in cash, boxing tickets, and support funding. The executives were fined 200,000 yen each.

Ito-Yokado. Three employees and three *sokaiya* were arrested in October 1992 for payoffs totaling 27.4 million yen. Two executives were sentenced to six months' imprisonment, suspended for three years. The third executive was found not guilty. One *sokaiya* was sentenced to four months' imprisonment, suspended for four years, and the other two were sentenced to six months' imprisonment, also suspended for four years.

All but one of those accused in these incidents received suspended sentences. The only case resulting in imprisonment was that involving Noritake, in which a *sokaiya* received a sentence of five months. Most fines ranged from 150,000 to 200,000 yen—although the payoffs made by the corporation could be many times that figure. The payoffs made to *sokaiya* ranged from 150,000 yen to the 27.4 million yen paid by the executives of Ito-Yokado, a major department-store chain.

Just why a particular company would make arrangements with *sokaiya* is never reported publicly. Executives who are convicted are usually required to resign their positions, but in many cases they simply find new employment in subsidiaries or related firms—albeit at lower levels and in less responsible positions.

Although the details of most of the above cases are largely unknown, the Ito-Yokado case was covered extensively in the press, and the judges' decisions were published in a special edition of *Shoji homu*, thus providing the opportunity to examine more closely the mechanics of the *sokaiya*-corporation symbiosis.

The Ito-Yokado Case

This case involved cash payoffs from three executives of Ito-Yokado Company, at that time Japan's second-largest supermarket chain, to three *sokaiya* representing three prominent *sokaiya* organizations, all with ties to Sumiyoshi-kai, a major organized-crime syndicate. Arrests were made on October 22, 1992, and all six persons (three *sokaiya* and three executives) were charged with violation of Commercial Code Article 497. According to the findings of the court handed down in February and March 1993, Yasuchika Saito, the auditor of the supermarket firm, Tomiyuki Sakairi, general manager of the securities section, and Ryuichi Tsumura, the general affairs manager, handed over a total of 27.4 million yen (about $274,000 at that time) to the *sokaiya*. In exchange, the three *sokaiya*—Kazuhiko Morita, a member of Rondan Doyu-kai (perhaps the largest and most well-organized *sokaiya* group known), Masao Tsuruno, leader of Seiran (a *yakuza-sokaiya* organization formed by Sumiyoshi-kai), and Noriyoshi Sakamoto, the leader of the Kawauchi-gumi gangster group as well as head of the *sokaiya* organization known as Morimoto Kigyo Chosa-kai (Morimoto Enterprise Investigation Group), also connected with Sumiyoshi-kai—were asked not to raise questions during the company's regular shareholder meetings. It has never been made clear what the questions would be about.

Rondan Doyu-kai traces its roots to the mid-1970s and the movement of Hiroshima gangsters into *sokaiya* activities. Today it is firmly connected with Sumiyoshi-kai. One source claimed in an interview that "the leader of the Rondan group is guarded day and night by Sumiyoshi-kai members. As you get near to his neighborhood, you will see men sitting in automobiles and standing around. They are Sumiyoshi guards who are the *sokaiya* leader's bodyguards." The fact that three *sokaiya* groups with the backing of a major crime syndicate received payoffs may explain, in part, the tremendous amount of money involved. The 27.4 million yen is in reality only a portion of the payoffs. Often these types of arrangements grow over the years, meaning the amount that actually moved from the company into the hands of the extortionists may be many times that reported by police.

According to the court, the Ito-Yokado executives were part of an ongoing payoff scheme on the part of the company's management to ensure quick, undisturbed shareholder meetings. At the May 28, 1992, meeting (for which the money was paid), the company's business reports were read and approved and the company's auditor was selected without incident. Of even more interest was the fact that this case was not the first instance of collusion between *sokaiya* and Ito-Yokado management. Since 1985, the court found, Ito-Yokado executives had been making payoffs as part of what was termed "shareholder-meeting countermeasures" (*kabunushi sokai taisaku-hi*). Saito, the auditor, was in charge of finding the money within corporate accounts, moving it into other secret accounts, and laundering the transactions to cover the payoffs. The court further stated:

> As the auditor, he was responsible for the operating and financial affairs of the firm and even though he should have stood guard against payoff demands, since he was also responsible for *sokaiya* countermeasures, he oversaw and agreed to the raising of funds and methods of hiding the transactions and therefore bears a heavy responsibility. ("Ito-Yokado reiki yokyo jiken saiketsu" 1993, 83)

Sakairi and Tsumura, the other Ito-Yokado executives, acted as conduits to the *sokaiya*. Money was exchanged on three occasions: the first payment of 1 million yen ($10,000) was made on July 13, 1992, to Sakamoto; the second payment of 13.1 million yen ($131,000) was delivered on July 21, 1992, to Morita; and the final payment, totaling 13.3 million yen ($133,000), was transferred to Tsuruno on July 28, 1992.

According to the court, the 27.4 million yen did not represent the total amount of corporate funds passed to these *sokaiya* since 1985. By Ito-Yokado's estimates, the court said, the known total was closer to 41.6 million yen ($416,000), but even that "is certainly not the entire sum" (ibid., 87).

The reaction to the Ito-Yokado case in the corporate community was one of deep interest—but deep interest only. Such a large payout, observers said, indicated that the *sokaiya* had discovered a potentially crippling scandal or misdeed by the firm. One *sokaiya*, however, argued the opposite: that the individuals involved on both sides simply had become accustomed to the idea of passing and receiving huge sums of money. Further, he believed, by paying out such a huge sum of cash to *sokaiya* groups with *yakuza* backing, the company essentially bought security against any other *sokaiya* who might attempt to take action against the firm at its shareholder meeting. As another *sokaiya* told an *Asahi shimbun* reporter:

> They get used to passing money around. There aren't any real secrets (that the firm is hiding) and Ito-Yokado is not a particularly negligent company. In general, they would not have been caught if the money had been less since most companies find it easy to hide payoffs of 100,000 yen or 200,000 yen [$1,000 or $2,000]. Those are small amounts and not much at all for a major company. However, their payment to these organizations purchased groups of men who would stand guard at the entry to the

shareholder meeting. One look at them and you knew they were violent men. It was very threatening. ("Ito-Yokado shacho jinin" 1992, 9)

Payment of a quarter million dollars annually to these three groups bought solid protection against other potentially troublesome *sokaiya*. However, because the payoffs were discovered, the effect on the company was just the opposite—scandal erupted where the firm's managers had hoped to avoid it. In the end, the president of the firm resigned as a sign of personal responsibility for the affair.

Notes

1. The following account was taken from a report by *Asahi Shimbun* reporters ("Sokaiya to kigyo no tantosha no daienkai" 1991, 9).

2. This data was provided by a detective within the Violent Group Countermeasures Section No. 2 of the National Police Agency. Information from this source is identified in the text by the abbreviation "VGC."

3. The Komin-to incident, as noted in the text, was never completely understood by the public, although many of the details of the affair, including the background and how it was eventually resolved, were reported. In particular, see Mizoguchi 1993, 116–25, and *Mainichi shimbun* 1992, 223–31.

6

Sokaiya at a Shareholder Meeting

In his examination of the social organization of extortion, Joel Best described that crime as being distinguished from all other predatory and exploitative crimes by the relationship existing between the perpetrator and the target:

> In extortion, the two actors strike a bargain: The extortionist threatens to injure a hostage unless the target agrees to pay a ransom. The particulars vary: The hostage may be a person (kidnapping), property (racketeering), or a reputation (blackmail); the extortionist and target may be individuals or groups; and the ransom, typically a cash payment, can take many forms, for example, the release of prisoners. (Best 1982, 107)

(For more on extortion and rackets, see Miller 1978.)

In this book we have seen that the "hostage" is reputation, either of an individual manager or of the corporation. Corporate management worldwide is sensitive to public image—Erving what Goffman terms its "face" or

> the positive social value a person effectively claims for himself by the line others assume he has taken during a particular contact. Face is an image of self delineated in terms of approved social attributes—albeit an image that others may share, as when a person makes a good showing for his profession or religion by making a good showing for himself. (Goffman 1969, 3)

This sensitivity to face has long been understood by those studying corporate affairs. John Maynard Keynes noted:

> A point arrives in the growth of a big institution . . . at which the owners of the capital, i.e. the shareholders, are almost entirely dissociated from the management, with the result that the direct personal interest of the latter in the making of great profit becomes quite secondary. When this stage is reached, the general stability and reputation of the institution are more considered by the management than the maximum of profit for the shareholders. The shareholders must be satisfied by conventionally adequate dividends; but once this is secured, the direct interest of the management often consists in avoiding criticism from the public and from customers of the concern. This is particularly the case if their great size or semi-monopolistic position renders them conspicuous in the public eye and vulnerable to public attack. (Keynes 1932, 314–5)

The corporation and its managers hope to avoid criticism because criticism could draw the eye of state regulators, who then might tamper with the operation of the corporation and threaten the position of the managers. Or, criticism may adversely affect sales or other corporate operations that managers use to justify the continuance of their positions in the company.

The managers, however, also attempt to maintain a good public image and solid standing among their friends and colleagues. American corporate gadfly Lewis Gilbert (with his brother John), much emulated by Japan's *sokaiya*, used the sensitivity of managers to outside criticism as a pressure point to goad management, publishing an annual review of corporations he monitored, and rating managers on their performance with regard to shareholders.

> Nowadays directors have regard for the published criticism of the Gilberts, because these might affect their public image. Arrogant behaviour, increases in salaries while dividends are decreased, unsatisfactory replies to questions put at an Annual General Meeting (AGM)—all these are not offences against the SEC, but when publicised adversely they become important to most directors, because they might tarnish their social standing in the community. (Rubner 1965, 124)

Common *Sokaiya* Tactics

How do *sokaiya* threaten the "face" of management and the targeted corporation? In addition to producing their own publications, which may contain articles critical of managers and their failings, they can challenge managers directly at shareholder meetings. Their challenges can come from a number of different directions. Tatsuo Osumi (1966) and Shinjiro Maeda (1968) have noted eight of the most widely used methods of attack:

1. Demands for the reinspection of the authenticity of shareholder seals. Seals are inked stamps usually of the Chinese characters representing the individual's name. They are mass- produced and one registers one's seal with the local municipality. A seal has much the same legal standing as signatures have in the West.

2. Questions about the completeness of management reports delivered by the meeting chairman or about reports on other corporate or management affairs.
3. Questions covering errors found or suspected in management reports.
4. Charges that accounting documents are too simplistic or do not cover the range of the company's assets.
5. Questions reflecting the incompetence or negligence of management.
6. Charges that management salaries or bonuses are excessive when compared with management performance or when compared to dividends paid to shareholders.
7. Calls for replacement of management or for the resignations of certain managers for the good of the company.
8. Complaints that entertainment expenses are too high and that management is wasting corporate resources (Osumi 1966, 205–6; Maeda 1968, 237–39).

All of the above are justifiable complaints that a shareholder in any society might raise. However, in Japan the key is not simply *what* issue is raised, but *how* it is raised. In shareholder meetings, *sokaiya* use tactics that other Japanese, particularly those involved in protest movements or social-conflict situations, use against what Susan J. Pharr (1990) calls "status superiors."

Verbal Confrontation

In her examination of several cases of social conflict in Japan, Pharr describes a pattern of confrontation similar to what is seen at Japanese shareholder meetings when *sokaiya* take the floor. This pattern involves those of lesser status engaging in forms of behavior usually reserved for individuals of higher status. She found that "as events escalate, status inferiors go beyond nonconformity to expected behavior and, in effect, turn the tables on superiors by laying claim to their very language and prerogatives" (Pharr 1990, 125).

This is more clearly demonstrated in the process of *kyudan* or "denunciation." *Kyudan* is a method of protest employed by *burakumin*, particularly members of the Buraku Liberation League, since the 1920s. In *kyudan* the *burakumin* group targets an individual who it feels has acted in discriminatory ways or contrary to the interests of the *burakumin* cause. They "kidnap" the individual, usually at his office or other public place, and proceed to harangue him until he admits his mistakes and promises to work for *burakumin* interests.

> The methods used in a session vary greatly according to the seriousness of the discrimination and the degree of resistance offered by the accused. It is common for Burakumin to shout, stamp the floor, use insulting language, make angry gestures, and dance and chant around the accused, creating a sense of chaos. (ibid., 127)

However, a *kyudan* session is not the only means by which Japanese can act out anger or express other strong emotions in unusual but socially acceptable ways. After-work drinking sessions with superiors are another common venue for socially acceptable outbursts. The workers may air their gripes, sometimes with great emotion, and it can be done in relative safety from reprisal, since, first, all involved are considered under the influence of alcohol and therefore largely blameless for their actions and, second, presentation of complaints is one of the purposes of these sessions.

For the manager who must sit and listen to a loud diatribe about problems in the department or section he oversees, such a session does not represent a loss of face; rather, it is a symbol of his concern and willingness to look out for the general well-being of the group. Moreover, he is able to demonstrate his authority not only by having the emotional stability to withstand heavy criticism by status inferiors, but also by taking serious note of the complaints and in some way attempting to relieve them.

In any verbal confrontation involving status inferiors and status superiors, the change in language that takes place is important. In effect, inferiors turn the tables on their superiors, using harsh forms of expression without the normal softening effect of polite forms of address. Several layers of polite language forms are available to Japanese in dealing with those above and below them in status. In nonconfrontational settings, these language styles are an expected form of expression, giving each participant cues to gauge their position.

In many social situations in Japan it is possible to determine the status position of those involved. For example, one might hear a man and woman speaking in so-called plain-form Japanese, indicating that they know each other well and are comfortable enough to engage in plain-form talk. If another associate joins the conversation, they might switch to a slightly more formal level (often described as the *masu* form, meaning the verb endings change to a more formal level), demonstrating that all know each other, but not well enough to use more casual grammatical constructions. Finally, if a status superior becomes involved, they may shift into more polite levels of talk (known as *keigo* or respect language), thus showing deference. At the same time, the status superior may use either an informal or formal level of language that denotes his relationship with the listeners.

Such shifting conversational levels of respect are done quite naturally and without conscious thought. In conflict situations, however, the shifts in language are purposeful and deliberate and are part of the resources participants use in verbal jousting.

Of course, these verbal resources are available to both sides in a confrontation.

As noted above, status inferiors often will turn the tables on status superiors in confrontational settings and use impolite language. Pharr noted that this resource was applied elsewhere. For example, in confrontation between university students and faculty and administrators,

> the language of superiors and inferiors was often turned upside down as students adopted the expressions used to dress down or wield authority over inferiors, while professors and administrators spoke in honorifics. Indeed, in such exchanges superiors typically became exceedingly polite in order to highlight the students' "rudeness" and to establish their transcendence of the situation [in] an attempt, actually, to reassert authority and control. (ibid., 129)

The use of increasingly polite levels of language by the authorities is important. To "lower" themselves by using the same form of language as their attackers would mean losing the confrontation, as this would demonstrate anger. "Losing one's cool," as we might describe it in the West, is interpreted as a direct loss of face.

> Coolness is exhibited (and defined) as poise under pressure. By pressure we mean simply situations of considerable emotion or risk, or both. Coolness, then, refers to the capacity to execute physical acts, including conversation, in a concerted, smooth, self-controlled fashion in risky situations, or to maintain effective detachment during the course of encounters involving considerable emotion. (Lyman and Scott 1968, 93)

This concept becomes exceedingly important in the context of shareholder meetings in which *sokaiya* verbally confront managers in public.

Shareholder-Meeting Confrontation

In the Japanese shareholder meeting, the person in charge of running the meeting—usually the corporation president or other high-ranking corporate officer—must remain cool, no matter what the attendees, especially *sokaiya*, do. Depending on the individual *sokaiya*, tactics may involve exceedingly polite but derisive questions, or, at the other extreme, may involve crudeness: for example, a blatant attack on the chairman's personality. Coarse language, thorny questions, taunts, jokes, and other verbal missiles usually considered inappropriate in a formal business setting must be endured and handled as if they had not occurred. That is, the chairman must remain cool in order to protect his personal face and that of the company, as he and the other corporate officers in attendance represent the public "face" of the firm.

Shareholder meetings in Japan are closed to the general public, as only managers or shareholders of the corporation have any real business to conduct there. However, some shareholder meetings are secretly tape-recorded by attendees who then sell the recordings to those wishing to study the meeting's conduct. These are far more effective reference materials than a mere transcript, which can never capture the full flavor of the meeting. These tapes are bought by a number of different people. They may be *sokaiya* targeting the company for future payoff approaches who hope to learn particular weaknesses of the corporate officers. Other buyers might be shareholder -meeting managers from other companies who hope to gain insight into the abilities of certain *sokaiya* and how best to handle their questions or disruptions. They may be played in order to prepare the meeting's chairman for what he might face, thus helping him to maintain his cool.

I obtained such a tape and will use it here to analyze how *sokaiya* disrupt a meeting. Although the meeting took place in the late 1980s, the man who gave it to me said it is a good representation of the effect *sokaiya* can have on a meeting. It shows how *sokaiya* use the tactics outlined by Maeda and Osumi earlier in this chapter, as well as verbal abuse in the form of taunts, jokes, and status-inferior language forms, against those normally considered status superiors. In response, managers used polite honorifics at all times.

The meeting began with some two hundred shareholders present, including eleven known to be *sokaiya*, who were identified as professional shareholders (*puro kabunushi*) in a transcript which accompanied the tape. Due to numerous disruptions, the meeting was exceedingly long, lasting one hour and fifty-four minutes. Speakers are identified by initials only. Notations to the transcript are contained in brackets, and these notations identify the progression of the meeting. Spoken words are in quotation marks. The following transcript includes the romanized version of Japanese all in uppercase letters followed by a basic English translation in upper- and lowercase script. In addition, I have included additional notations that mark particular forms of disruption as well as verbally abusive language.

Finally, the transcript in no way gives the full flavor of the meeting as demonstrated on the tape recording of the proceedings. At times it is difficult to make out spoken words, as there are other shareholders, probably *sokaiya*, shouting near the tape recorder and other background noise which further affects the poor quality of the tape.

Shareholder-Meeting Transcript

10:14 A.M.
[IKKATSU KAITOO NI HAIRU.]
[General responses.]

GICHOO: "OSHIZUKA NI, GOSEISHUKU NI."
Chairman: "Please be quiet. Silence, please."

[GIJOO SOOZEN TO NARI IKKATSU KAITOO NO SETSUMEI GA YOKU KIKITORENAI JOOKYOO.]
[Conditions in the hall become so noisy that the explanation of the summary of responses is inaudible.]

Here, the meeting chairman, who is also the company president, attempts to bring order to the hall. He uses polite forms of grammar construction to address the audience. Some in the audience ignore him for some time, but they eventually settle down to listen to his report, omitted here for brevity. At 10:32 A.M. the meeting is open to questions from shareholders. Under normal conditions, the majority of Japanese shareholder meetings would conclude about here, some thirty-two minutes after opening.

Complaints are raised about the company using employee shareholders to block questions and comments from shareholders. Usually, according to corporate insiders, managers who fear confrontations with *sokaiya* flood their meetings with employees who are also shareholders, and often they are the largest male employees available. It is not clear, in any case, whether these employees bought their shares for investment purposes or were required to purchase the shares in order to gain admittance and act as extra security. It would be an interesting legal question, never raised in the courts, whether the use of corporate employee shareholders in meetings is, like the use of *sokaiya*, a violation of the Commercial Code, since the exercise of shareholder rights on behalf of the corporation is a precondition to being an employee shareholder.

10:32 A.M.
[SHITSUGI OOTOO NI HAIRU.]

[Questions and answers begin.]

[O, Y, K, T-RA NI YORI SHAIN KABUNUSHI NI TSUITE MONKU.]
[Complaints raised about employee shareholders by sokaiya *O, Y, K, T, and others.]*

10:33 A.M.
["ZAITEKU WA TEIKAN IHAN" TO IU H TO GICHOO TO NO YARITORI NO NAKA DE "KANREN SHITSUMON" TO O NADO GA HATSUGEN SHI, TEEBURU WO HIKKURIKAISU OTO NADO MO ARI GIJOO WA SHUUSHUU NO TSUKANAI JOOKYOO.]
[During an exchange between H and the chairman about "financial engineering as a violation of articles of incorporation," O and others shout out that they have "relevant questions"; there is the sound of a table being overturned and circumstances reach a point where it is impossible to get order in the hall.]

[GICHOO WA SHIKIRI NI "SEISHUKU NI" "SOO IUU TAIDO WO TOTTARA TAIJO SASERU" TO ITTE SEISHI SURU GA KOOKA WA NAKU GIJO WA SOOZEN TO NARU.]
[The chairman frequently calls for "Silence" and says, "If you maintain that behavior, I'll have you thrown out," but to no effect and the meeting hall becomes noisy.]

The meeting is in disarray for nearly fifteen minutes. The chairman is unable to establish order, asking for questions that are relevant to the business at hand. *Sokaiya* O charges that manipulation of assets (known as *zaiteku* in Japanese) is a violation of the articles of incorporation. *Zaiteku* is known interchangeably in English as "financial engineering" or, less often, as "financial technology" and refers to any financial transaction including stock and foreign-exchange speculation. (See Kester 1991, 222–27, for a discussion of *zaiteku* and its uses in the late 1980s when this shareholder meeting took place.) This is the first instance of the use of one of the standard tactics mentioned by Osumi and Maeda—that is, that management's activities may be negligent since a violation of the articles of incorporation could potentially harm the corporation's legal status and open it up to state prosecution or lawsuits by shareholders. *Sokaiya* O is not polite, using a lower form of expression, calling the chairman incompetent and claiming that he is losing control of the meeting and of his own emotions. Other unidentified *sokaiya* chime in with taunts and jibes, reinforcing *sokaiya* O's attempts to raise the chairman's ire.

10:50 A.M.
[SOKAIYA O, *SHIME WO UKERU.*]
[Sokaiya *O is recognized.*]

SOKAIYA O: *"GIJI UNEI NI KANSHITE HONTO NI WARUI YO ANATA WA. KABUNUSHI-SAN WO KORE DAKE OKORASETARA DAME DAYO."*
Sokaiya O: "You're rotten when it comes to running the meeting. It's no good if you're gonna get angry with the shareholders just for this kind of thing."

GICHOO: "KANREN SHITSUMON WO OSSYARU TO IU NO DE SHIME SHITAN DESU."
Chairman: "You were recognized because you said you had a relevant question."

SOKAIYA O: "HAI, KANREN SHITSUMON. KOCHIRA NO KABUNUSHI KARA NO SHITSUMON WO UKETE NO

KOTAE TO SHITE, YUUSHI WO UNYOO SURU NO GA SHIGOTO DESUTTE ITTA NE?"
Sokaiya O: "Yes, a relevant question. Regarding your answer to the question from this (unidentified) shareholder, you said that making investments was something that could be considered work, didn't you?"

GICHOO: "SOO IU KOTO WA MOSHIMASEN!
Chairman: "I said no such thing!"

SOKAIYA O: "ITTA JYA NAI KA?"
Sokaiya O: "You didn't say that?"

[EIGYOGAI NO KINYUU YUUSHI NI TSUITE.]
[Topics related to financial investments unrelated to business.]

["ZAITEKU WA ZETTAI YAMERO!" "MUNO NA KEIEISHA WA YAMERO"!]
[Unidentified voices: "Quit financial engineering!" "Get rid of inefficient managers!"]

Once again the meeting falls into disarray while a second *sokaiya*, *sokaiya* I, takes the microphone for questions. He charges that the chairman is displaying bad manners toward shareholders by leaning on the podium with his elbows instead of standing erect. The chairman makes matters worse by fumbling a response to a question on financial-asset manipulation and attempting to explain that he is not leaning on his elbows. *Sokaiya* I engages in a series of crude remarks, as if speaking to a person of no consequence. *Sokaiya* O yells that the chairman seems like nothing more than a bumbling gardener. The interruptions continue, and the chair attempts to defend himself. His ability to remain cool is slipping. Finally *sokaiya* I asks that the names of shareholders be checked (another traditional tactic), but the attempt at verification is dismissed by the chairman.

[GICHOO NO "ZAITEKU WA SHIGOTO" TO NO SHITSUGEN WO NUGUTTE SHITSUGI OOTOO GA TSUZUITA NOCHI, I-SAN GA SHIMEI WO UKERU.]
[The chairman's misstatement that "Financial engineering is work" is passed over and after some questions and answers, sokaiya I is recognized.]

SOKAIYA I: "HITO GA SHITSUMON SHITEIRU NO NI HIJI WO TSUKUNA."
Sokaiya I: "Even though people are asking questions, you're leaning on your elbows."

GICHOO: "KORE WA KONO DAI (TSUKASA) NO KANKEI DE KOKO WO TSUKANAI TO KYORI GA AIMASEN NO DE KESHITE HIJI WO TSUITEIRU NO DE WA GOZAIMASEN. TSUGI NO GO-SHITSUMON GA ARUNDESHITARA. . . . SHITSUMON GA NAKEREBA HOKANI MAWASHIMASUYO."
Chairman: "I can't even reach the top here. I'm not leaning on my elbows. If you have another question. . . . If you don't have a question I will turn to the next person."

SOKAIYA I: "KOTAETE NEE JYA NAI KA?"
Sokaiya I: "You're not answering, are you?"

GICHOO: "IMA OKOTAESHIMASHITA."
Chairman: "I just answered you, sir."

SOKAIYA I: "NANTE ITTANDA. KIKOENAYO. MO IKKAI ITTEMIRO."

Sokaiya I: "What the hell did you say? I couldn't hear. Let's hear you one more time."

SOKAIYA O: "ONIWA NO SOOJI WO YARU NO?"
Sokaiya O: "Do you think you're working in a garden?"

11:09 A.M.
GICHOO: "SO IU KOTO WA HON SOOKAI NO GIDAI NI SOGUWANAI KEREDO, TONIKAKU HONGYO DE KAISHA WO YOKU SURU YOO NI WATASHI WA DORYOKU ITASHIMASU. MO0 ICHIMON GOZAIMASU KA? TAKUSAN IRASHYAIMASU NO DE GUTAITEKI NI KANKETSU NI HAYAKU ONEGAISHIMASU."
Chairman: "That has nothing to do with the proceedings of this general meeting and in any case I am working hard to do the best for this company. Do you have another question? Since there are many others I ask you to speak concretely, briefly, and quickly."

[KYAKU KABUNUSHI GA HATSUGEN OMOTOMETE GIJOO FUNKYUU.]
[Numerous shareholders demand to speak, throwing the hall into confusion.]

GICHOO: "SEISHUKU NI!"
Chairman: "Silence!"

SOKAIYA I: "KONO ATARI NI IPPAI KABUNUSHI GA IRU DARO. SAKKI ANATA WA ZENBU IPPAN KABUNUSHI TO ITTARO. ITTAN DASHITE MEIGI GA ATTEIRU KA, IPPAN KABUNUSHI KA DOO KA, SHAIN KABUNUSHI KA DOO KA, CHEKKU SHITE MIROYO."

143

Sokaiya I: "There are a lot of shareholders here. Just before, you said that all of them are regular shareholders. If that's the case, let's check their names and see if they're regular shareholders or company shareholders."

GICHOO: "SONO HITSUYO WA NAI TO OMOIMASU. KORE DE KONO MONDAI WAS UCHIKIRI. SUGI NO SHITSUMON NI UTSURITAI TO OMOIMASU."
Chairman: "I don't think that's necessary. With that, that problem is closed. I think I would like to move on to the next question."

The following statements and questions by *sokaiya* K regard the accuracy of corporate reports, another traditional tactic. The long-winded preamble not only is designed to take time, but it helps him set up suspicions about the effectiveness of management's investment policy and financial engineering, something management was doing without shareholder approval. The *sokaiya* focus on this because they can make an argument that funds are being hidden or improperly invested.

When the chairman turns the responsibility of answering the questions to the managing director, several *sokaiya* hurl more epithets at the chairman. *Sokaiya* K raises the level of abuse by using the chairman's name without the honorific "*san*" and by addressing him with the lowest form of "you" (*"teme"*) available to a Japanese. Again, the language is crude and ill mannered.

When the managing director also fumbles his answer with inaccurate cost figures on real-estate acquisition as part of a corporate-expansion program, he is berated by *sokaiya* K in much the same manner that the managing director might berate an incompetent underling. Although other *sokaiya* continue to disrupt the meeting, *sokaiya* K demonstrates a higher level of skill by taking apart the company figures and forcing management to explain complicated financial details. For *sokaiya* K, this is a standout moment. He not only disrupts the meeting, but demonstrates his competency and prowess by engaging in crude baiting as well as incisive questioning and debate, even while other *sokaiya* are raising a ruckus.

11:11A.M.

SOKAIYA K: "SAKIHODO KARA SHISAN UNYOO NI KAN SURU IRON NA II IKEN GA DETERU. MOCHIRON WATASHI MO SOO IU FUU NA KATACHI DE TOOSHA WA SOO IU UNYOEKI WO AGETEIRU TO SAISHO WA OMOIMASHITA. SHIKASHI, EIGYOO HOOKOKUSHO TO KA YUUKA SHOOKEN HOOKOKUSHO TO KA FUZOKU MEISAISHO WO TORIYOSETE YOKU SHIRABETEMIRU TO, CHYOTTO GIMON NI OMOU TEN GA DETEKITAN DE SONO TEN NI TSUITE NANI IMASU. MAZU EIGYOO HOOKOKUSHO NO SAN PE-JI NO SETSUBI TOOSHI NO RAN NI JYUGO (15) OKU GO HYAKU YONJUKYU MAN EN NO OMONA MONO TO ARIMASU GA, KORE WO GUTAITEKI NI SETSUMEI SHITE KUDASAI?"

Sokaiya K: "Just before, there were some good opinions which came out about asset manipulation. It's true that I thought from the beginning that, in the same way, I would like to see the investment profits of this company rising. However, when I obtained and carefully checked the management report, financial statement, and the attached detailed statements, some questions came out and I believe I would like to hear a bit about these points. First, the management report on page three in the facilities investment column shows a principal amount of 150,49,000,000 yen. Could you please give a concrete explanation of this amount?"

GICHOO: "SAKIHODO NO IKKATSU KAITOO DEMO OKOTAESHIMASHITA NO DE CHOOFUKU SURU KAMO WAKARIMASENKEREDO, SENMU NO M KARA MOO ICHIDO OKOTAESASEMASU."

Chairman: "Since this was answered previously during the general response, I think we might be repeating ourselves, but I will have Mr. M, the managing director, explain one more time."

SOKAIYA K: "(CHAIRMAN), TEME WA NANI MO KOTAERARENAI NO KA, KONO BAKAYAROO GA! TEME WA HIRUNE TO GORUFU SHIKASHI RA NEE NO KA?"

Sokaiya K: "Can't you answer anything, you stupid idiot! Don't you know anything except naps and golf?"

SOKAIYA Y: "SORE WA SOOMU NO SEKININ DA YO."

Sokaiya Y: "That's the responsibility of the general affairs department."

SOKAIYA T: "WATASHI GA KAWARIMASHYOOKA."

Sokaiya T: "Let's change to me."

SOKAIYA O: "FUSHIGI GA ARU YO. NANI MO SHIRANAIN DA MONO."

Sokaiya O: "It's unbelievable. He doesn't know anything."

SENMU M: "W. SHUCHOOJO NO TOCHI WO SHUTOKU ORIMASU. W. CHIZU NI KIBOO NO HAMBAISHO WO SETSURITSU SURU TAME NO SOCHI DE GOZAIMASU."

Dir. M: "It's the cost of the acquisition of the land for the W. prefecture branch. It is a step in the establishment of a retail store as shown on the W. map."

SOKAIYA K: "KINGAKU WA?"

Sokaiya K: "How much money?"

SENMU M: "SAN OKU AMARI DE GOZAIMASU."
Dir. M: "Some 30 billion yen."

SOKAIYA K: "NI OKU SANSEN NANA HYAKU MAN EN
DESHYOO. SEIKAKU IITTE KUDASAI."
Sokaiya K: "Twenty-three billion, seven million yen. Please
speak with exactness."

SENMU M: "CHYOTTO MATTE KUDASAI."
Dir. M: "Wait a moment, please."

SOKAIYA T: "OI, OI. SHIKKARI SHIROYO."
Sokaiya T: "Hey, hey. Be firm."

SOKAIYA O: "DAME DA YO, M-SAN."
Sokaiya O: "That's no good, Mr. M."
SOKAIYA K: "SAN-GATSU NI HAKKO SHITA SHINKABU
HIKIUKE-KEN TSUKI NO RISOKU WA YON TEN
NIJYUGO PACENTO (4.25%), 297 OKU NO 4.25% WA
TANJUN NI KEISAN SHITEMO 12 OKU 7 SEN MAN EN
NAN DESU YO. YAHARI KOKO DEMO KYU OKU NO
OKANE GA KIETEIRU WAKE YO."
Sokaiya K: "The cost of underwriting the new shares in March
carried a charge of 4.25 percent. Four and a quarter percent of
297 billion roughly calculates to 12.7 billion yen. It would ap-
pear that 9 billion yen is missing."

SENMU M: "KIMATSU DE WA TASHIKA NI SOO IU
KEKKA NI NATTEIMASU GA, KICHU NI WA TANKI
KARI-IREKIN MO ARIMASU SHI, SONO ZANDAKA
DAKE DE KEISAN ITASHIMASU TO SOO IU KEKKA NI
NARIMASU."

Dir. M: "If you calculate your figures at the end of the term, certainly that's the result, but in mid-term we had short-term loans and if one uses that balance only for your calculations you get that result."

SOKAIYA K: "YUURYOO KAISHA GA DOOSHITE WARIBIKI RYO WO HARATTE MADE TEGATA WO WARANAKEREBANARANAIN DA?"
Sokaiya K: "Why must a superior company pay a discount rate on its promissory notes?"

SENMU M: "WARIBIKI RYO WA SAN TEN NIJYUGO PACENTO (3.25%) NO RE-TO DE WARHIITEIMASU."
Dir. M: "The discount rate was 3.25 percent."

GICHOO: "K-SAN NO SHITSUMON WA KORE DE UCHIKIRITAI TO OMOIMASU."
Chairman: "I believe I want to end Mr. K's questions there."

Sokaiya H is recognized. Unlike *sokaiya* K, *sokaiya* H is rougher and even more belligerent, although he couches his remarks and questions by saying he is a supporter of the company and is willing to do what it takes to accomplish the business at hand. He moves back over old ground, hitting the company on asset manipulation. At one point, he suggests the chairman is a thief.

Then, approximately forty minutes into the meeting, the chairman looses his cool. He previously stated that asset manipulation (*zaiteku*) is not actually work, but now reverses himself and calls it work entrusted to management by the shareholders, although clearly shareholders were not consulted about this. *Sokaiya* O, seeing an opening, attempts to jump in, but is rebuffed by the chairman. *Sokaiya* O uses this to make another joke about the chairman being overly sensitive.

Sokaiya H regains the initiative after *sokaiya* O's interruption, but instead of staying on the topic of asset manipulation, he suddenly changes tack, asking for details about the major shareholders of the firm. He wants them identified. Caught off guard by the sudden shift in questioning, the chairman hesitates and seems confused, making matters worse.

Such "major shareholders" are a form of cross-shareholding in which companies purchase each others' shares, thereby cementing relations between the firms and adding a defense against any outsiders since the major shareholders are considered "safe shareholders" (*anzen kabunushi*) who will always vote with management. Asking for a verbal identification of the major shareholders is a variation on the traditional *sokaiya* tactic of verifying shareholder identifications (mentioned by Osumi and Maeda).

[SOKAIYA H SHIMEI WO UKERU.]
[*Sokaiya* H is recognized.]

SOKAIYA H: "YATTO MODOTTEKIMASHITA. MOO SUKOSHI HAYAKA NI YATTE KUDASAIYO. WATASHI WA HITOTSU SHITSUMON SHITA DAKE NANDESU YO. HAETTEKURU NO NI ICHIJIKAN NIJYU-PUN KAKATTEIRU WAKE DESUYO. MOCHIRON R. NO TAME DESUKARA, TETSUYA DEMO NAN DEMO GANBARIMASU KARA MINASAN MO GANBATTE KUDASAI NE. ZAITEKU NO MONDAI DE MOO ICHIDO, ZAITEKU WA SHIGOTO DE WA NAIN DESUKA, SHIGOTO DESU KA?"

Sokaiya H: "At last you came back to me. Be a bit quicker please. I have only one question. That's because an hour and twenty minutes has already passed. Of course I'm for [the company] so if it takes all night or however long I'll persevere. Everyone please be patient. Once again it's financial engineering; Is financial engineering not work or is it work?"

GICHOO: "ZAITEKU WA HONGYOO DE WA GOZAIMASEN."
Chairman: "Financial engineering is not regular work."

SOKAIYA H: "ANATA WA DOROBO WO SHITEIRUN DESUKA?"
Sokaiya H: "Are you a thief?"

GICHOO: "YUSHI NO UNYOO WO SURU NO GA WAREWARE NI MAKASARETA SHIGOTO. . . . SEKININ DA TO OMOIMASU."
Chairman: "Using investments is the work you leave to us. . . . I think it's our responsibility."

SOKAIYA O: "ANTA WA SOSOKKASHIIN DA YO!"
Sokaiya H: "You're careless!"

GICHOO: "H-SAN NO SHITSUMONCHU DESU KARA O-SAN WAS SUWATTEKUDASAI."
Chairman: "Mr. H is asking questions, so Mr. O, please be seated."

11:26 A.M.
SOKAIYA O: "OSETSUMA DE HANASHITEIRUN JYANAIN DAKARA OCHITSUITE HANASHINASAYO. SHII—NANTE IU WO ABUNAIN DAKARA NE."
Sokaiya O: "We're not talking in a parlor, so calm down. Gee—you're in trouble, no matter what you say."

SOKAIYA H: "IMA UNYOO SHITEIRU TO IIMASHITAYO NE. ZAITEKU WA SHIGOTO JYANAI KEREDO [THE COMPANY'S] NO OKANE WO UNYOO SHITE RIEKI WO ETA MONO WA SHIGOTO DE WA NAI WAKE DESUKA?"
Sokaiya H: "You just said the word 'using,' didn't you? Even though financial engineering may not be work, are you saying that moving [the company's] money to get profits is not work?"

GICHOO: "EIGYOOGAI TOSHITE."
Chairman: "Outside regular business."

SOKAIYA H: "JYAA, GICHOO GA IU KOTO GA MOTTOMO DA TO OMOTTE IPPO SAGATTE UNYOO TO SHIMASHYOO. [THE COMPANY'S] NO OKABUNUSHI WA DOKO DESUKA?"
Sokaiya H: "Well then, the chairman has spoken, so let's take one step back. Where are [the company's] major shareholders?"

GICHOO: "OOKABUNUSHI TO IU NO WA?"
Chairman: "Major shareholders?"

SOKAIYA I: "OKABUNUSHI MO SHIRAN NO KA?"
Sokaiya I: "You don't know the major shareholders either?"

SOKAIYA T: "SOKUTOO SHIRO!"
Sokaiya T: "Answer promptly!"

GICHOO: "SEIMEI HOKEN, GINKOO, TORIHIKISAKI TO KA TAKUSAN GOZAIMASU NODE. ICHIBANME, SUMITOMO SEIMEI; NIBANME. SUMITOMO GINKOO; SANBANME, SUMITOMO SHINTAKU GINKOO; SANBANME. . . . YONBANME, MITSUBISHI GINKOO;

GOBANME, MEIJI SEIMEI . . . "
Chairman: "Life insurance companies, banks, other companies with business connections. . . . Number one, Sumitomo Life (insurance); number two, Sumitomo Bank; number three, Sumitomo Trust and Banking; number three . . . number four, Mitsubishi Bank; number five, Meiji Life . . ."

SOKAIYA H: "RIEKI WO TSUIKYU SURU AMARI ACHIKOCHI NO KABU WO KATTEIRU. OSEIWA NI NATTEIRU TOKORO NI 'R.' NO RIEKI WO MOTTEIKUNARA MADA GAMAN GA DEKIRU GA, ZENZEN KANKEI NO NAI KAISHA NO MONO MADE KAIASATTEIRU."
Sokaiya H: "In the pursuit of profits you purchase shares all over the place. I can deal with buying shares of companies with some connection to our company, but those without any connection at all can't be permitted."

GICHOO: "SOOIU SHOOSAI NA KOTO NI TSUKIMASHITE WA MOSHIAGERAREMASEN."
Chairman: "I am unable to provide those kinds of details."

The meeting ended at 11:54 A.M. following several similar disruptions, including questions about fixed assets and the possibility of a subsidiary-firm listing on the stock exchange. With the end of questioning, votes were cast on pending bills. The bills were approved and the meeting concluded.

The activities and behavior of the *sokaiya* at the meeting may seem tame to Westerners, as they are accustomed to harsh debate and, among those with somewhat combative personalities, welcome open conflict, even in public. But for the high-level Japanese executives who run these types of meetings, the jokes, jibes, insults, crude talk, and other disruptions exhibited by the *sokaiya* at this meeting are the most appalling form of behavior to endure.

According to insiders who consult with companies about the conduct of their shareholder meetings, there is no real way to determine what topics will be raised by *sokaiya* at any time. Some indications can be gleaned from conversations with major *sokaiya* hired as consultants and who are so well connected that they receive a constant stream of rumors about companies. In addition, managers are usually aware of weak points in their corporate performance and, in private briefings, determine the best way to deal with responses to any questions that might arise.

However, when it comes to the more crude tactics employed by *sokaiya*, much depends on the character of the chairman of the meeting and his supporters, usually upper-level managers and members of the board of directors. According to insiders, since the late 1970s, it has become increasingly common for companies to hold rehearsals prior to an actual shareholder meeting. Scripts are developed and coached answers are reviewed. Often, non-*sokaiya* consultants are called in to handle such rehearsals, in cooperation with managers and subordinates in charge of the basic operation of the meeting.

Several consultants have said, however, that they must provide their own people who serve as *sokaiya* actors during the rehearsals—an indication that *sokaiya* verbal abuse is so repulsive that no employee is asked to role-play as *sokaiya*. If the rehearsal is to be effective, the verbal abuse must be heavy. Employees, despite understanding it is a rehearsal, find it impossible to speak to their status superiors using language that would only be used toward a status inferior.

Consultants, then, most often turn to retired police officers who used to work in the violent-group-investigation bureaus of local police departments. Such men are used to dealing with

sokaiya, *yakuza*, and other toughs; they know how gangsters talk and how to pressure and aggravate corporate officials used to being addressed in only the most polite forms
of speech. Since they work for the consultant, they owe no
loyalty to the company or the corporate officials to be
abused.

A form of this work was portrayed in the Japanese movie
Minbo no Onna, directed by Juzo Itami, who himself was attacked by gangsters. The movie concerns a female lawyer who
fights extortion cases and serves as a consultant to a hotel targeted by a local crime syndicate. *Minbo* is an abbreviation for
minji kainyu boryoku or violent intervention in civil affairs (see
chapter 7), and covers all forms of extortionate or otherwise
violent activity in matters which should be handled either in a
court of law or through arbitration.

In the movie, the hotel employees crumble under the verbal
abuse of the gangsters. In order to toughen them up, the lawyer
brings in a large, frightening individual who begins to unleash a
stream of abuse on them. It becomes apparent later that he is a
police officer who deals with organized-crime matters. The lawyer teaches the employees how to remain cool in spite of this intimidating person's speech, and she reinforces the idea that doing
so not only makes them a stronger force, but maintains the integ-
rity of the hotel as well. If one loses one's temper, she explains,
that also can be used by the gangsters in complaints to management that the employees are weak or rude.

Ultimately, the employees learn from her, stand firm against
incredible pressure from the gangsters, and save the name of
the hotel. But life is not always as it appears in the movies.

7

Riding the Bear

When Juntaro Suzuki, the vice president of Fuji Photo Film, was killed on the doorstep of his home, the incident was more than simply a bizarre murder. A one-time sokaiya *handler for a major Kansai-based manufacturing company had said it would be only a matter of time before such an incident took place. If Suzuki had not been at home that night, he said, then someone else—such as Mrs. Suzuki—would have been a suitable target. The victim was not of great importance.*

"Remember," the manager said, "everything a sokaiya *does is related to building up his reputation. Every time they appear at a meeting it is noticed. Every time they cause a disturbance, the news about that disturbance will spread. They probably didn't mean to kill him. Cutting him badly would have been enough. Or if it was his wife, that would have been just as effective, especially cutting her on the face. That's a popular tactic. The point is the message would have been clear to everyone."*

And many such messages are sent. Terrorist attacks against Japanese executives and their corporations became increasingly common events in the first half of the 1990s, although they are seldom reported in the West. In recent years, firebombings, stabbings, and slashings, and at least three execution-style slayings, including that of Suzuki, became a growing part of the corporate scene. The perpetrators who are caught are often members or associates of right-wing political groups with ties to gangster organizations, *sokaiya*, or small-time gangsters.

Part of the reason for the increase in violence lies with the collapse of Japan's so-called bubble economy, an era of hyperinflation in which overvalued real estate, securities, and other investments were used as collateral for loans to purchase more overvalued investments. By the early 1990s, the bubble was bursting, sending the Japanese financial system into a panic. As of this writing, the system is still trying to recover through new regulations and temporary fixes.

The rapid readjustment of a pathologically hyperinflated economy reached its first peak at the same time the Violent Group Countermeasures Law or Boryokudan Taisaku-ho, (hereafter Botaiho) took effect. The law was designed to serve as a major counterforce to the long-standing practice of using gangster organizations to settle disputes. In other nations, such problems would be settled within the relatively safe confines of a courtroom, before a judge or jury. In Japan, however, a local gangster may act as judge, jury, and, in some cases, executioner.

The combination of forced austerity by companies (following nearly a decade of mounting paper wealth during the bubble's inflation) and legal restrictions on organized-crime activities curtailing valuable sources of illegal income resulted in a bloody campaign of terror against corporations and managers.

The Bubble Economy

The so-called bubble economy had its roots not in Japan but in the United States, where President Ronald Reagan attempted to deal with a Congress calling for increased protectionist measures against the Japanese. The Reagan plan argued that by weakening the dollar against other currencies such as the yen, prices of imported goods would rise and curb U.S. appetite for foreign products. At the same time, U.S. exports would become more attractive to foreign buyers because they would become cheaper (Uekusa 1991, 23).[1]

In September 1985, the Plaza Agreement was signed by the five leading industrial democracies. It called for coordinated intervention in the currency markets in order to adjust the exchange rates of those nations' currencies against the U.S. dollar. In February 1985, the dollar was selling for 260 yen; by January 1988, the same dollar bought only 121 yen—a 53 percent devaluation. This devaluation led to lower interest rates in Japan, from 5 percent to 2.5 percent by February 1987. The drop was triggered by an export slump (due to higher prices for Japanese goods) and a general economic slowdown in the Japanese domestic market. Lower interest rates have a countereffect in securities markets and other markets prone to speculation, such as real estate and investment art, by driving up the value of these assets. By 1987, the Nikkei stock average doubled in value, from 12,500 points to more than 24,000, and then continued upward to 38,915 points on December 9, 1989 (ibid., 24–25).

Land prices also began to rise out of all proportion to their value. In 1985 the total value of all residential land in Tokyo was estimated at 176 trillion yen, compared with an estimated gross domestic product (GDP) of 324 trillion yen. Economists believe such a ratio would be appropriate for long-term sustainable growth in Japan's postwar economy—that is, investment in real estate could be counted on to increase in value at a certain rate (assuming some minor fluctuations). Investments could be made on relatively predictable assumptions about the value of those investments. Slight declines and advances in the value of investments could be tolerated.

However, when those trends become unpredictable by shifting into wide swings in value, that investment can go one of two ways. If large slumps take effect, investment tends to decline, because investors fear a depression and a loss in the value of their holdings. If the economy becomes hyperinflated, investors tend to see potential profits in their investments through capital gains. If the value of property increased 10 percent one year and conditions did not change, then another 10 percent could be realized the following year. In other words, buy now, but get out before the trend takes the predictable fall back to "normalcy."

By the end of 1987, the value of residential land in Tokyo grew to more than 1.5 times the Japanese GDP. Similarly, the total value of shares reached to the equivalent of the nation's GDP in 1988 and continued to expand in 1989. By definition, a hyperinflated or bubble economy exists when the portion of a price increase in real estate or securities is in excess of past overall trends in the economy. Japan's bubble economy was a classic case where all rules of the past three decades appeared to have dropped away, and investors saw others becoming rich overnight, leading them further into the market as well (Noguchi 1994, 8; Taniguchi 1993, 19–23).

But speculative bubble economies do not take place by themselves. Indeed, they are driven by the actions of people who themselves are driven by a false belief that the rise in asset values will continue without stopping. Or, far more common, the bubble-economy investor comes to believe he or she has special insight into the workings of the market and will somehow be able to predict the best time to get out while the getting is still good, possible, and, most of all, profitable.

In Japan, banks began lending money for the purchase of real estate as individuals and corporations attempted to enter the boom. The reduction in available real estate inevitably drove prices higher. Those who hoped to make a killing in the market used the assets they already owned—already valued at inflated prices—to finance further lending. The boom continued until the loans came due. As one economist has pointed out, "[P]rices cannot go on rising eternally. At some point, they must crash: This is an absolute. And the greater the speculation, the greater the crash" (Okumura 1992, 60).

Prices of land and securities plummeted as those who were overextended in loans faced default. Banks and securities companies could no longer afford to ignore the nonperforming loans on their accounts. From its December 31, 1989, high, the Nikkei plunged to about 16,000 (48 percent) by October 1, 1990. Twenty-one Japanese banks reported between $51 and $59 billion in nonperforming loans (loans where no interest is being paid on the principal). Some analysts said the true figure was probably closer to $154 billion but was kept hidden by lax banking regulations, a time lag on reporting nonperforming loans, and loans created in a secondary market through nonbank credit organizations (Taniguchi 1993, 2; Wood 1992, 21–47).

The second-tier market was seen as severely overextended. Largely unregulated by the finance ministry and backed by the false security of their parent firms (the major city banks and large cash-rich corporations such as Toyota), these credit organizations—similar to credit unions in the United States—went on a loan-making binge. Between March 1989 and March 1990, the top two hundred nonbank loan organizations increased the number of their loans by 47 percent. In the same period, Japanese banks increased their loans by 12 percent. Nearly half of the new nonbank loans went to property companies and construction companies—that is, Japanese investors were able to expand the bubble further by side-stepping banks and going to the second-tier market (Wood 1992, 39).

Among those participating in the buying binge were crime syndicates, which saw an opportunity to launder money in the market through the creation of dummy corporations, sales of golf-club memberships (costing tens of thousands of dollars), and land-development schemes. The syndicates took advantage of easy stock purchases and the added security of trading houses willing to cover losses. Thus criminal syndicates were among those cut off from new loans when the bubble burst and the first drops of cold water began to fall on the overheated economy. And like other lenders, they were expected to make good on their outstanding debts, the lenders' assumption being that criminal syndicates operate just like everyone else—they pay their debts (ibid.). Even as lenders felt the first pangs of panic, a new law took effect that was designed to curtail organized-crime-group operations and put pressure on gangster incomes. Even if criminal syndicates intended to make good on their debts, it would become less easy because of the new law.

The Violent Group Countermeasures Law

With the enforcement of the *Botaiho* in March 1992, organized-crime groups confronted a new obstacle that could be used either to prevent their penetration of legitimate markets in order to launder their money or to dominate existing illegal markets where their services were sought and appreciated.

Japanese citizens are not necessarily reluctant to use the courts to settle civil disputes. However, the hurdles built into the Japanese civil-court system make the use of the courts costly, time-consuming, and unsatisfactory in terms of resolution. The average Japanese is more likely to rely on dispute resolution through informal and extralegal negotiations to settle civil matters normally handled by courts and lawyers in the West. They will seek out intermediaries to act as go-betweens. Among those who might serve as intermediaries in Japan are local temple priests, schoolteachers, and, at times, members of organized-crime syndicates. The practice of *yakuza* involvement in the settlement of civil disputes led to the creation of a new crime category called *minji kainyu boryoku* (violent intervention in civil affairs), better known as *minbo*.

Minbo is not a crime in itself. Rather, it is a category for crimes in which violence or the threat of violence is used to interfere in disputes that could otherwise be handled through the courts or through formal or informal mediation. In December 1979, The National Police Agency (NPA), followed by the Japan Federation of Bar Associations in March 1980, created their own definitions of *minbo* crime. Both organizations also established consultation centers where individuals could get advice about dealing with such violent intervention. However, the definitions of *minbo* and the services provided by the two groups are somewhat different. The NPA will take action only in those cases where a group deemed violent interferes in civil disputes. Bar association members will handle all cases where violence or the threat of violence is involved.

The bar association is critical of the police definition, as the designation could be applied to groups such as unions or other noncriminal organizations where members become involved or have been involved in violent confrontations. However, the bar association also holds that violence is not an option in civil disputes and will handle any case in which violence or the threat of violence is employed. If a labor union and company were to become involved in violent confrontations, the bar association would be willing to intervene and attempt to mediate the dispute, regardless of charges brought by the prosecutor against any individual.

The bar also warned that the law provided the police an opening into civil disputes that could be used to overstep police bounds (Nihon Bengoshi Rengokai 1986, 3). Such police intervention is a departure from a postwar policy of broad nonintervention in civilian disputes. The original postwar policy of nonintervention was formulated as a response to heated criticism by civilians of the use of force reminiscent of prewar police activities to quell disturbances. Following brutal repression of protesters in mass demonstrations in the mid-1950s, police were forced to change their tactics.

From then until now, the Japanese police, while maintaining a heavy presence in the community by a variety of means, including the famous *koban* system of police boxes, are generally reluctant to intervene actively in a situation until public opinion indicates they can do so without risk of public criticism (Katzenstein and Tsujinaka 1991, 141–66). This reluctance extends downward from mass protests and civil conflicts to the arrests of debtors at the behest of creditors (Nihon Bengoshi Rengokai 1986, 6).

Types of *Botaiho* Violations

Under the law, the local public-safety commission (*koan iinkai*) can designate a group as violent when the group's members establish a pattern of violent behavior resulting in the arrest and conviction of one or more of the members. The commission does this by examining the arrest records of group members. Once a group is designated violent, and an allegation of violence or the threat of violence is lodged by a citizen, the police can order the designated group to cease all such activities. If the order is ignored, arrests and dispersion of the group may take place (Keisatsucho Boryokudan Taisakuho Kenkyukai [KBTK] 1992, 1–7).

The *Botaiho* somewhat resembles in form and content the American Racketeer Influenced and Corrupt Organizations (RICO) Act passed by Congress in 1970. The RICO Act, however, is broader in scope because it identifies as one crime any series of crimes committed by a criminal group. Beyond dispersion as in the Japanese case, the RICO Act exacts stiff penalties including imprisonment of up to twenty years or life, fines ranging from $25,000 to $500,000 or twice the gain or loss suffered by a group's victim, and forfeitures, injunctions, and treble civil damages (Kennedy and Finckenauer 1995, 318–23).

What types of crimes are involved? In most cases this means extortion (*kyokatsu*), but carried out in different ways. Besides *sokaiya*, the following types of criminals and their activities are covered by the law.

Seiriya intervene in corporate bankruptcies, either as creditors or at the request of a creditor, and use lawful and unlawful means to act as a bankruptcy adjuster. They usually have power of attorney and take control of the company seal, registration, credit certificates, and other papers. They might also fabricate credit claims to get payments in a settlement or short-term-lease rights of equipment or other property, which they then hold as payment on outstanding debts. Because of their familiarity with bankruptcy laws and regulations, they might be called in to protect a company's credit standing.

Jidanya help with out-of-court settlements of traffic accidents on behalf of one party. Once they receive payment, they sometimes, albeit rarely, fabricate a dispute with the party for whom they were working and keep the entire settlement for themselves.

Toritateya are similar to *seiriya* in that they most often act for creditors to collect debts. However, a debtor may hire a *toritateya* to silence demands from a creditor. In these cases also a dispute may be fabricated so that the *toritateya* can keep all recovered funds for himself.

Pakuriya and *sarubejiya* involve themselves in the use of promissory notes. The *pakuriya* defraud their victims by saying they would like to examine the note, then keeping it. Occasionally they tell their victim they can get a rebate on the note, but never turn over payment for it. *Sarubejiya* offer to recover notes taken by *pakuriya*, but at a premium price. *Pakuriya* and *sarubejiya* have been known to cooperate with each other.

Apatoya usually employ an accomplice, often a seemingly non-threatening female. The accomplice rents an apartment; when rent is not paid, the owner is confronted by the accomplice's "boyfriend," who announces he is a member of this or that crime group and refuses to pay the rent. Then he begins to cause trouble throughout the apartment building, making loud noises, threatening neighbors, and so on. The trouble ends only when the accomplice is paid by the owner to leave the apartment.

Thousands of cases of violent-group interventions have been reported since the establishment of the police-consultation centers in each of the nation's prefectures and major cities. For example, 1,150 violations of the law were reported to police in 1981. By 1990, the public reported 3,094. A similar increase in reported incidents can be found in each category, including problems with cash loans, credit accounts, down-payment refunds, real-estate problems, promissory notes, and company bankruptcies (National Police Agency 1982, 112; 1991, 116).

One informant, a lawyer deeply involved in anti-organized-crime activities, reported that a *yakuza* intermediary is particularly helpful to have on one's side in such disputes:

> If we [lawyers] become involved, you have to pay us 10 percent of the estimated cost at the start of the legal process. Then you must continue to pay for services as the suit progresses. So you

must be able to afford the suit before instituting one since there is no such thing as a contingency fee basis for carrying out a common civil suit. On the other hand, if you hire a *yakuza*, he will charge you a flat fee of about 50 percent of the total amount of money recovered and he will probably take only a few weeks to settle the case. A case through regular legal means could take years. (Interview 1994)

When asked what would stop the *yakuza* from keeping all of the money, the informant laughingly said that doing so would ruin his reputation; hence it would be in his interests to treat his client fairly. Another lawyer, Ishiba Masatsugu, who was once an organized-crime investigator for the police, claimed: "When the courts or the civil law system do not function properly, a corrupt system expands. The underground society is a reflection of the society above ground" (*Mainichi shimbun* 1992, 227).

Minbo lawyers have likened the *Botaiho* to "trying to shoot down an F-16 with a bow and arrow." However, the law apparently caused many organized-crime syndicates to revamp their methods of operation in order to maintain steady income, although it overlapped with general belt-tightening among corporations due to the recession following the collapse of the bubble economy. Many corporations became more cautious about payoffs to groups and individuals, attempting to cut back on the huge sums of money paid out to buy peace. As the payoffs decreased, criminal groups, including *sokaiya*, increased their levels of violence against errant corporations who attempted to reorder the rules governing their past relations.

Unintended Consequences: The Suzuki Slaying

The enforcement of *Botaiho* and the collapse of the bubble economy, along with the Commercial Code reform of 1982 and the lessening of payoffs to *sokaiya* and other organized-crime groups, provide the necessary background for understanding the murder of Juntaro Suzuki, mentioned at the beginning of this chapter.

Suzuki began managing Fuji Photo Film's shareholder meetings in 1992. At the time, Fuji Photo controlled approximately 70 percent of Japan's color-film market and was targeting the international market that was dominated by Eastman Kodak. The firm also was one of the fewer than two dozen companies holding its shareholder meetings in January, forgoing the advantages of group protection accorded to those companies holding their meetings on the same day in June.

According to statistics on shareholder meetings collected by the legal journal *Shoji homu*, Fuji Photo's meetings were running well beyond the average of firms holding shareholder meetings in January. Its 1991 meeting, held the year prior to Suzuki's assuming shareholder-meeting management, ran for forty-two minutes—nearly double the average twenty-seven minutes recorded by all companies in January that year. At the time, *sokaiya* were already targeting the firm for disruptions, and the company managers either had not arranged for *sokaiya* protection, or their payoffs were insufficient to cover all threats.

Once Suzuki took over, the meetings grew even longer. The 1992 meeting lasted sixty-three minutes, while the average for all firms was thirty-one minutes. The following year the average fell to twenty-nine minutes, but Fuji Photo's meeting lasted 113 minutes. Finally, in 1994, while meetings overall lasted an average of forty-seven minutes, Fuji Photo's dragged on for an astounding 262 minutes ("Kabunushi sokai gaikyo—Ichigatsu sokai" 1992; "Kabunushi sokai gaikyo—Ichigatsu sokai" 1993; "Kabunushi sokai gaikyo—Ichigatsu sokai" 1994)—the obvious conclusion being that *sokaiya* were disrupting the meetings, asking questions, and forcing management to provide increasingly detailed explanations of actions and policies. Clearly, something had changed once Suzuki took charge.

Interestingly, despite its stranglehold on the domestic color-film market, Fuji Photo reported reduced profits and falling sales. One reason for this was the disposable-camera market. While the cameras were very popular with Japanese consumers, thus boosting unit sales of film (one measure of market domination), the disposable-camera bodies were unpopular with developers, thus forcing the company to initiate a collection service to remove them—an added cost and a drain on any profits. Consequently, Fuji Photo was criticized for employing such a costly method to boost film sales and market share (*Japan Company Handbook* 1994, 408). However, the disposable-camera issue need not have been particularly costly; instead, it was merely an effective topic an intelligent *sokaiya* could use for extended discussions at the firm's shareholder meetings.

Convincing top management to undergo the humiliation of questioning by *sokaiya* is one of the most difficult things a shareholder-meeting manager can get top management to do. There are few people who want to stand in front of a room full of shareholders and be subjected to the abuse that a group of *sokaiya* can pour on him. Top management consists of men who hold extremely prestigious positions; for years their employees and colleagues have treated them with respect every day.

One *sokaiya* reported that before Suzuki took over the firm's *sokaiya* operations, Fuji Photo had been paying out about 100,000 yen (approximately $1,000) each to forty or fifty *sokaiya* every year. Suzuki, with management's consent, ended that practice, which was when trouble began. One of the *sokaiya* groups cut from payoffs was a particularly violent gang that had been operating in Kansai since the 1970s. The group's leader, a powerful *sokaiya* in his own right, was also a high-ranking member of Yamaguchi-gumi, Japan's largest crime syndicate. According to police, this group was probably involved in attacks against individuals working at six companies in the Kansai region around Osaka. However, group members were arrested for only one incident, involving the assault of an executive of Wacoal Corporation, a prominent lingerie manufacturer based in Kyoto. The leader was arrested on June 20, 1994, less than ten days before the annual shareholder meetings of 2,008 Japanese companies. The arrest allowed police to detain the leader before charging him until after the shareholder meetings. That kept him away from meetings and forced him to miss one of the most important days in the work year of a *sokaiya*.

As of this writing, police have been unable to link the group to another attack that took place in September 1993, although detectives say privately that they are certain the group was responsible. In that case, a female relative of the president of another Kyoto clothing manufacturer was attacked. As in the Suzuki killing, a man came to the door of the president's home claiming his car had struck a surrounding wall. The woman came out to inspect damage, whereupon the man slashed her face with a knife.

Such attacks, while unusual, indicate the lengths to which *sokaiya* will go to force a company into complying with their demands. In most cases, causing a disturbance or asking difficult questions is enough. In fact, disrupting Fuji Photo's shareholder meeting had been the pattern employed by the suspect group, and following Suzuki's arrival, each successive shareholder meeting became increasingly chaotic as *sokaiya* became more violent. The 1994 meeting, however, was exceptional in itself. Prior to the meeting, approximately twenty *sokaiya* stood outside the meeting hall, preparing themselves. One man sang a song about a character named Ashigarayama Kintaro, who meets a bear and rides him through the mountains. The meaning was clear: Fuji Photo, founded in Ashigara city, would, like the bear, be ridden until it paid.

Suzuki's Final Shareholder Meeting

The 1994 meeting began with a management report by the corporation's president. *Sokaiya* harassment began immediately, with shouts of "Die, die!" coming from the crowd of shareholders. *Sokaiya* asked question after question. Finally, one man, a member of the suspect gang, threw three one-shot whiskey bottles at the president; police arrested him. (The thrower had also thrown bottles at managers at the Shin Nihon Seitetsu [Nippon Steel] and Toyo Shintaku Ginko [Toyo Trust & Banking] meetings.)[2] Prior to the meeting, Suzuki had taken the precaution of assigning the first four rows to company shareholder employees. They had attempted to close the meeting several times by standing and shouting "No objections!" followed by applause, but the *sokaiya* nevertheless continued to raise questions and abuse the directors for some four and a half hours, until the company shareholders finally were able to end the meeting.

Aftermath

Experts who follow *sokaiya* activities believe Suzuki paid for this particular meeting with his life. He was causing just too much trouble by arranging for cuts in payoffs to *sokaiya*. His murder served as a reminder of what thwarted *sokaiya* were capable of doing and what might await any manager (or his family) who tried to end payoffs.

By June 1994, the country was entering the usual "*sokaiya* season" and the nation's newspapers were running their usual series of articles about *sokaiya*. But because of Suzuki's death, this year was decidedly different.

After the *Mainichi shimbun* ran a four-part series on *sokaiya*, it printed an editorial once again calling for companies to cut the links to *sokaiya*. The newspaper stated: "There has never been a year where so much attention is being given to shareholder meetings as this one. . . . Companies are now facing the question of whether or not they can actually end the unnatural marriage between them and *sokaiya* which has existed for so many years" (*Mainichi shimbun* 1994, 5).

The editorial noted that *sokaiya* had long enjoyed a safe haven within corporations where they provided a number of services to management. The 1982 Commercial Code reform presumably ended this relationship, making it illegal for management to provide payoffs to *sokaiya* for the exercise of shareholder rights. However, corporate managers still made payments to *sokaiya*, because *sokaiya* were increasingly turning to terrorist tactics to extort money, especially after the bubble-economy burst and companies tightened belts after three years of recession. Further, with the passage of the 1992 *Botaiho*, *yakuza* organizations were turning away from traditional sources of income (drugs, prostitution, and gambling) to economic crimes, which, when properly handled, are less open to detection. Legislation was creating new dilemmas as fast as it was resolving different ones.

The editorial warned that foreign shareholders representing major financial institutions were becoming an increasing presence in Japan. These had experience as active participants in the development of corporate policies. They were used to the spirited give-and-take of foreign shareholder meetings and therefore would not tolerate shareholder meetings that ended quickly with calls of "No objection." Embarrassing foreign criticism would likely increase.

Finally, it was noted that even the police were changing their attitude toward companies. Now police were willing to overlook past associations with *sokaiya* "if a company is going to make an earnest attempt to cut its ties to *sokaiya*."

Given these developments, the editorial stated, "We expect managers to have the guts to make a resolute stand against *sokaiya* and never give in to the pressure."

Such pronouncements, colored with the call to have "guts," belie the facts. Few managers, given Suzuki's killing, would risk the wrath of *sokaiya* desperate or willing enough to raise the stakes to such a high degree in their extortion campaign.

For the police, legal reform, arrests, fines, and the threat of prison had little effect on corporate managers faced with either linking themselves to a *sokaiya* or suffering what that *sokaiya* might do to them or the company. Consequently, a change in tactics was in order.

Notes

1. The engineering of the devaluation of the dollar and how this was first reluctantly accepted and then enthusiastically employed by Japanese financial institutions is detailed in Burstein 1988, 128–64. For a more journalistic account of the creation and bursting of the bubble economy, see Wood 1992.

2. In the early 1990s, Toyo Shintaku Ginko (Toyo Trust and Banking) ranked as Japan's fifth-largest trust bank. It is headquartered in Tokyo and was founded through the consolidation of the trust divisions of Sanwa Bank, the defunct Bank of Kobe, and the securities-management division of Nomura Securities (*Japan Company Handbook* 1994, 1125). Shin Nihon Seitetsu (Nippon Steel) held at that time the top domestic share of crude steel sales. The company was nonetheless facing a current-account deficit and increased cost-cutting measures (ibid., 471).

Epilogue

In the final moments of an interview with an Osaka-based *sokaiya*, as we sped in his Mercedes from a nightclub in the fashionable Ashiya district bordering a pre-earthquake Kobe, I asked why there is a peace-at-any-price philosophy (*koto-nagareshugi*) among corporation managers regarding *sokaiya*. After all, I said, there are no *sokaiya* in the United States but U.S. corporations are concerned about their reputations and their profits. They want to avoid scandals and public knowledge of management mistakes. Bad news of any kind can have a bad effect on the corporation.

He gave the question some thought and then repeated what I initially suspected was a simplistic answer, one that was heard from police, lawyers, and other gangsters when asked the same question: "Japanese companies are dirty," he said. "If they acted within the law, there would be nothing to question them about."

At that time, I was not satisfied, believing it was a flippant answer to what the *sokaiya* must have considered a naive question. In the end, however, he and all the others must be given their due. They were at least partially correct.

In the years since research for this work concluded and its

writing began, Japanese corporations have been shaken by huge scandals including many involving *sokaiya* and other elements of the Japanese underworld. For example, Japanese banks and securities companies were found to be linked with organized-crime syndicates through *sokaiya* Ryuichi Koike. By the time police investigators finished, they were able to piece together a mosaic of corruption involving Koike and the managers of leading Japanese financial institutions including Nomura Securities, Dai-Ichi Kangyo Bank, Daiwa Securities, Nikko Securities, and Yamaichi Securities. Nearly two dozen top managers of these firms resigned. Koike received uncollateralized and largely uncollectable loans from Dai-Ichi Kangyo Bank totaling some $250,000. The money from that loan and others was used to buy shares in the securities companies. At one point Koike held 300,000 shares of Nomura stock and threatened to raise embarrassing questions at its June 1995 shareholder meeting. Nomura managers paid him $340,000 to remain quiet. At the same time, Koike benefited from a special account designed to prevent any losses on his investments made through Nomura. In effect, the company would cover any losses he suffered from investments made with the Nomura firm.

The Koike case is not the only one to come to light, but it is representative of the dreary sameness that taints all of these affairs involving Japanese companies and *sokaiya,* back to the earliest known incidents at the end of the nineteenth century.

We arrive where we began. Why do *sokaiya* exist? The *sokaiya*'s answer above does not really explain the situation fully. The answer is much more complex, as I have tried to argue in this study. Any solution to the question needs to be parceled out if we are to have a good understanding of the issue. We will attempt to do that here by breaking the answer into some of its major parts.

Culture and "Face"

Unlike their counterparts in the West, who generally are willing to fight their accusers, Japanese managers, being Japanese, carry the concept of "face" to a higher level of importance and do not necessarily see "face" as limited to their individual public selves. The reputation of the firm and of those involved in it is of far deeper concern than, for example, career, family, individual and group reputation, potential legal troubles, lawsuits, unwelcome government investigations, and so on. As the sociologist C. Wright Mills long ago argued, personal troubles link directly to public issues and are not easily separated (Mills 1959, 8–11).

It is well known that in Japan, following the revelation of a scandal, Japanese managers will resign in order to assume responsibility for the embarrassment as in many of the cases cited above. Western managers, on the other hand, will more likely stay and fight and, even if they resign, it is not necessarily on behalf of anyone except themselves. However, once a Japanese manager or his underlings are caught in a scandalous situation, they have no other choice but to resign so that the many others who are dependent upon them do not take the blame or suffer any of the consequences:

> When something goes wrong [in a company] the senior man or group of men presiding over the mistake will "take responsibility" to lift the blame from their subordinates. Symbolic responsibility, which for the individual is simply the price of status, has some value for the company community. It encourages a conscious mutual dependence of seniors and juniors. Those below know that those above will protect them. Those above must rely on their subordinates not to make mistakes that will lead to responsibility having to be taken. When a mistake is made the

resignation, transfer or other penance of the leader of the group allows everyone to make a fresh start. (Clark 1979, 125–6)

However, in the cases examined in this book, the most damaging scandals and mistakes grew out of intentional acts of wrongdoing and seldom out of mismanagement. Lines separating right action from wrong were consciously crossed by managers who were willing to make illegal payoffs to *sokaiya* who themselves were all too willing to make illegal demands for payoffs. Still other *sokaiya* took on roles in Japan where regulatory agencies such as the Federal Securities and Exchange Commission or, in the private sector, corporate lawyers would assume roles in the United States (discussed below). So even though the concept of "face" as a culturally based force driving personal action is a powerful idea, it alone is far too simplistic an explanation of the *sokaiya* phenomenon. Other factors—beyond culture—are involved that grow out of Japan's corporate history and law, as well as its social structure.

The Extortionate Contract

A second element that must be examined is the relationship existing between the extortionist and the extorted. It is not merely one of perpetrator versus victim. The extortionist and the extorted enter into a sort of contract to protect a hostage. As long as the ransom is paid, the hostage is not harmed. In this study, the reputation of the firm is the usual hostage. But why is that an issue? Why does extortion exist at all in this situation?

In the early years of modern Japanese corporate development, the lack of limited-liability laws required corporation owners to ensure their own survival since their personal wealth was at stake. Without limited liability, in which the wealth of the corporation and not its managers was the only thing at stake, owners and investors were in a position of constant threat of financial ruin. A hint of scandal could persuade investors to run from the firm. This weakness alone was enough to tempt predators. The fundamental conditions of the extortionate contract were in place.

The extortionists and the extorted, therefore, entered into a working agreement regarding the health and welfare of the hostage—in this case the reputation of the company (and of course the personal wealth of the extorted). This extortionate contract did not end with a single payment. It is the nature of extortion to continue through ongoing demands for payments. We saw that Japanese businessmen were not prey to a single extortionist or extortion group. Some companies doled out money to dozens of individuals, finding it easier to make such payments than to deal with the headaches that might be caused by resistance.

But company managers were not powerless in this situation. They could take action too. It was sometimes in their best interest to arrange for their own protection. And who better to fight extortionists than other extortionists?

We saw that through the hundred or so years of Japanese corporate history, firms have been willing to depend on "the devil you know" to protect them from "the devil you don't." This willingness to collaborate with the seedier elements of society for protection is a well-known fixture of political life in Japan. The use of gangsters and fixers by the powerful is well documented. It takes place to such a degree that to suggest an alternative to this process would appear ludicrous to a practical Japanese politician. The same goes for the practical Japanese businessman. So it is no wonder that one of the original founders of the *sokaiya* profession emerged from the political world where he served as a lobbyist. Such a person would understand how to pressure and threaten, how to destroy reputations and protect them as well.

Even though alternatives to this type of protection have been offered by the Japanese state over the years—in the form of changes in law and cooperation from the police and judiciary—these resources were generally rejected or went largely unused. The *sokaiya* were simply far more effective and reliable and there was no danger that corporate secrets would become government knowledge. There is some evidence for this in the way *sokaiya* developed a hierarchy among themselves with the top and most respected positions going to those who formed close relationships with corporate managers. Their help was not only sought in terms of defending management at a shareholder meeting. They provided further assistance through consultative services including, in at least one case, the selection of a corporate president. Thus the relationship between extortionist and extorted grew beyond this simple give-and-take situation and gathered depth through the years. *Sokaiya* were not and are not simply perpetrators. They are collaborators as well.

Informal "Legal" Services

In this sense, there is some parallel to be found between *sokaiya* in Japan and lawyers, especially corporate lawyers in the United States, who can play out all sorts of maneuvers to protect a client or further a client's interests short of litigation. These may include the writing of letters, representing clients at meetings, pretrial motions, and so on. In this sense, a lawyer is willing to show the client's hand just enough in the hope that the other party will fold and negotiate a settlement without resorting to the exposure of information in a civil court.

In their own way, *sokaiya* follow a similar pattern of work, hoping to show their hand just enough to convince the other side that they indeed have damaging information. They may threaten to publish it in a newsletter, reveal part of it in conversations with the firm's *sokaiya* handlers, announce it with the use of a pseudo right-wing propaganda campaign, and so on. The firm may employ the services of other *sokaiya* to defend the corporation and "work a deal" between the parties so that the scandal is covered up.

The last resort open to *sokaiya* and management is risking the exposure of damaging information at the shareholder meeting. Management must weigh how much harm could be done to the firm if a scandal is revealed. *Sokaiya* in possession of potentially damaging material have to weigh how much harm they can cause, given the pressure that might be applied to them by the authorities.

The reputation of the firm remains the primary focus. Share price is important of course. As one writer noted: "The higher a company's share price in Japan, the higher its status" (Alletzhauser 1990, 288). So scandal that could hurt the share price of a firm is dangerous. But it does not mean the company would necessarily be hurt just because the share price drops. The comfortable cushion of cross-shareholders and banks holding most of a company's shares makes even a major sell-off a rather momentary event. Reputation is worth far more. For example, after the president of the Mitsukoshi department store was ousted following a number of personally ordered corporate misdeeds, the price of Mitsukoshi stock plummeted. But more important, the reputation of the firm was so tarnished that shoppers went elsewhere to buy those luxury items that the store sold. The public did not want to have a connection to the store. Exorbitantly marked up gifts for New Year and other occasions, wrapped in distinctive Mitsukoshi paper, no longer held the same cachet.

Change and Adaptability

Also important to the ongoing strength of *sokaiya* within the Japanese corporate system is their adaptability to changes in the law. As pointed out earlier, organized criminal groups not only rely on their use of culturally driven behaviors, but must also be adaptable to modern changes in the social structures and systems in which they operate. Adaptation to legal change is therefore crucial to continuity.

What is remarkable is the way the changes in the legal system were not only adapted to but became a new resource for those in the system, including *sokaiya*. For instance, after the Allied Occupation following World War II, *sokaiya* and others were able to use the changes in disclosure laws to act against corporations. One purpose of these changes, instituted largely by American reformers, was to open the operations of corporations to greater scrutiny by potential and existing investors. Information that was once secret and closely guarded by corporate managers was now available to the common shareholder.

Until these reforms, the Japanese corporate manager was almost entirely uninterested in the opinions of the small investor. As the Allied reform investigators found, the small shareholder was never considered very important in the running of the corporation. Although small shareholders did become involved in corporate investment in the years after Occupation reform, that never really took hold and the system gradually drifted back to institutional investment as the main source of shareholder capital. The status and position of the shareholder in Japan remains fundamentally different from that in the West.

> [T]he common stock shareholder of the Japanese company is more in the position of a preferred shareholder in a Western company. Having made an investment that is at risk, the shareholder

is entitled to a return on that investment. . . . Yet when the shareholder's claim to a return on his investment is met by the Japanese company, the shareholder has little or no further voice in corporate affairs. (Abegglen and Stalk 1985, 184–85)

There are a number of reasons for this limiting of shareholder participation in corporate governance. These include a board of directors drawn almost entirely from the firm's senior management. If there are outside members, they will be farmed in from other firms in the parent group to which the firm belongs. The board's chief responsibility is to the company's employees. Their job is to ensure the continuance of the firm's place in the Japanese market. Without that, there will be no firm (ibid.).

Sokaiya, on the other hand, are not interested in control of the corporation. They are interested in the collection of information and the use of that information to generate payoffs. As we saw, the Allied reforms opened up new sources of information that could be used against management. This required management to react. Rather than limiting *sokaiya* effectiveness by increasing shareholder democracy, *sokaiya* power grew even as small-shareholder participation receded in the decades following the war.

The 1982 Commercial Code reform is another example of *sokaiya* adaptability and turning what could have been a setback into an advantage. As intended, the reform caused some reduction in the total *sokaiya* population. But this reduction was largely on paper, as some *sokaiya* did not meet the new minimum requirements for the exercise of shareholder rights set out in the reform package. Those who failed to meet those requirements did not automatically leave the *sokaiya* field. Instead, they pursued new avenues of extortionate behavior by forming into pseudo right-wing groups, adopting the guise of *burakumin* civil-rights organizations, or concentrating on the less profitable but nonetheless important work of newspaper and newsletter publication. While not strictly *sokaiya*, their targets remained the same and were a valuable source of pressure for the *sokaiya* working inside the meetings.

Finally, the legal reforms against violent intervention in civil affairs (the so-called *Botaiho*) presented new adaptive opportunities as well as hurdles. Private citizens as well as corporations could seek protection and assistance from the police in civil matters. This included blocking *sokaiya* demands for payoffs.

However, nothing changed. There is no evidence that widespread use of the law is being made at the corporate level. Instead, it appears that Japanese corporations are being driven further into a corner. Asking for help from the state would open up the corporation to the possible revelation of scandalous or illegal behavior by management. At least with *sokaiya*, managers know that payoffs will keep private matters private. Why invite in the authorities? After all, they are not engaged in achieving the goal of the extortionate relationship: the protection of the company's reputation.

At the same time the *Botaiho* took effect, the bubble economy burst. The time of overinflated wealth and profiteering reversed into belt-tightening and austerity. Indiscriminate demands for payoffs were less welcome and, in some cases, the reservoir of payoff money that was once doled out so freely grew dry.

This combination of legal and economic changes more than likely cemented further the relations existing between corporate managers and the more powerful *sokaiya* who could, like a well-trained security force, keep other *sokaiya* at bay. But it also shows that *sokaiya* are extremely adaptable to changes in the law. In some way, every legal change designed to eliminate or stymie *sokaiya* activities was in fact successfully circumvented.

Ties to *Yakuza*

Ties to the more traditional and larger organized-crime syndicates in Japan—collectively known as *yakuza*—strengthened the position of *sokaiya* in the corporate system in the last half of the twentieth century.

Extortion rackets, especially protection rackets, were never a major source of *yakuza* income. Most syndicate-crime profits derived from vice rackets such as narcotics, gambling, prostitution, and pornography. These profits were large and steady until the 1960s. At that time, *yakuza* organizations, especially those centered in Tokyo, came under intense police crackdowns. This was due to the negative reaction of government and political leaders to the move by the ultranationalist Yoshio Kodama to unite far right-wing political groups with mainstream gangster organizations under a single political entity in support of the Liberal Democratic Party (LDP). It was true that LDP leaders appreciated the muscle brought by Kodama's followers during struggles with left-wing opposition forces, especially during major conflicts over the Japan–U.S. security treaties. But it was also true that they did not wish to share power with gangsters and ultrarightists in running the government. They further understood that even the most politically tolerant segments of the Japanese voting public would not tolerate a clear and open association between their political leaders and criminal gangs.

The crackdowns of the 1960s saw the arrests of hundreds of *yakuza* figures, including top-line leaders. This disrupted syndicate chains of command. Younger leaders unexpectedly found themselves in authority positions many years sooner than they expected. Also, the traditional forms of *yakuza* profit were severely disabled under police pressure. The *sokaiya* field presented a unique opportunity to branch into a new line of profit and at the same time offered the young leadership an opportunity to exercise control over a new area of power.

Simultaneously, the golden age of the prewar *sokaiya* leaders, in which a few hundred *sokaiya* could make a comfortable living off cooperative corporations, was coming to a close. The so-called lone wolves of that era were being replaced by younger and more aggressive leaders who understood that there was a quicker and more profitable response when a corporate manager was faced with "violence and numbers."

The hybrid breed of *yakuza-sokaiya* became a standard fixture of the *sokaiya* world in less than a decade from the mid-1960s to the mid-1970s. From a few hundred *sokaiya* known to be operating in Japan in the 1960s, the *sokaiya* population mushroomed to several thousand.

For the *yakuza*, this was a perfect situation. With very little effort, hundreds of *yakuza* could now make a living by extorting money from corporations. The money was safer than any other form of illegal income in that corporate managers were very reluctant to call in the authorities for protection (if the thought ever crossed their minds at all).

Older, aging *sokaiya* leaders also found a positive side to the incursion of *yakuza*. Ties to *yakuza* organizations brought additional muscle in times of physical confrontations, such as in the cases of the antiwar and antipollution protests. But also the linkage brought additional control in power struggles in and out of *sokaiya* organizations. As we saw in one of the early standoffs between an established *sokaiya* group and a *yakuza-sokaiya* group, high-ranking gangster leaders served as intermediaries. The old *sokaiya* was able to maintain his position and leadership while the younger *yakuza-sokaiya* was able to achieve a strong and recognized position in the *sokaiya* field. But at the center, dominating the entire process, were *yakuza*.

In the last decades of the twentieth century, the *yakuza-sokaiya* network served to broaden and deepen underworld penetration into the mainstream corporate system. Scandal after scandal revealed that it was no longer merely corporate managers paying off pesky *sokaiya*. Now *sokaiya* and managers were cooperating with *yakuza* in elaborate schemes involving investments and loans and straight protection deals in order to avoid questions about other potentially scandalous activities.

Any Solution?

Newspapers and magazines in Japan continue to produce articles about new scandals involving managers of powerful corporations involved in unsavory relationships with gangsters, including *sokaiya*. As mentioned before, these stories have a dreary sameness about them—in a way, read one, and you have read them all. There seems to be no end.

Could the Japanese government put an end to *sokaiya* involvement in corporate affairs? Aside from very drastic measures and legal reforms, there is no imaginable way the relationship between corporate managers and *sokaiya* could be cut. As seen in this study, *sokaiya* are just too useful to managers who require certain services that no one else in Japan can supply in the way *sokaiya* supply them. And *sokaiya* are just too skilled in manipulating the system in which they operate to be removed by mere changes in law. They probably would view any such move by the authorities as an amusing challenge.

What would be absolutely necessary for the removal of *sokaiya* would be a fundamental change in the consciousness of the Japanese corporate manager. He would have to be able to put aside any consideration of the firm and his working group and the damage that might be caused to them. He would have to open up his company to outside scrutiny by the authorities and risk having important secrets exposed. He would have to begin listening to shareholders at shareholder meetings. He would have to view any challenge raised by any shareholder at any time to be what the *sokaiya* once were to him—a necessary evil.

References

Abegglen, James C., and George Stalk, Jr. 1985. *Kaisha: The Japanese Corporation*. New York: Basic Books.

Alletzhauser, Al. 1990. *The House of Nomura*. London: Bloomsbury.

Ariyama, Keiichi. 1980. *Kabunushi sokai to kigyo boei kyogikai* (Shareholder meetings and corporate defense associations). Osaka: Ariyama Trade Service.

Baldwin, Frank. 1974. "The Idioms of Contemporary Japan VII: *Sokaiya*." *The Japan Interpreter* 8, no. 4: 502–9.

Berg, Lisa, and Lasse Berg. 1971. "Stockholders' Corral." *Ampo* 9: 54–55.

Best, Joel. 1982. "Crime as a Strategic Interaction: The Social Organization of Extortion." *Urban Life* 11, no. 1: 107–28.

Bisson, T.A. 1954. *Zaibatsu Dissolution in Japan*. Berkeley: University of California Press.

Burstein, Daniel. 1988. *Yen!* New York: Ballantine Books.

Catanzaro, Raimondo. 1985. "Enforcers, Entrepreneurs, and Survivors: How the Mafia Has Adapted to Change." *British Journal of Sociology* 36, no. 1: 34–57.

Clark, Rodney. 1979. *The Japanese Company*. New Haven: Yale University Press.

Curtis, Gerald L. 1975. "Big Business and Political Influence." In E.F. Vogel, ed., *Modern Japanese Organization and Decision-Making*, pp. 33–70. Berkeley: University of California Press.

DeVos, George, and Keiichi Mizushima. 1967. "Organization and Social Function of Japanese Gangs: Historical Development and Modern Parallels." In

R.P. Dore, ed., *Aspects of Social Change in Modern Japan*, pp. 289–325. Princeton: Princeton University Press.

Drucker, Peter F. 1975. "Economic Realities and Enterprise Strategy." In E.F. Vogel, ed., *Modern Japanese Organization and Decision-Making*, 228–48. Berkeley: University of California Press.

Edwards, Corwin D. 1946 "The Dissolution of the Japanese Combines." *Pacific Affairs* (September): 227–40.

EHS. 1991. *The Commercial Code of Japan* (vol. 2). EHS Law Bulletin Series. Tokyo: Eibun-Horei-Sha.

Ferrel, Jeff, and Clinton R. Sanders. 1995. "Toward a Cultural Criminology." In J. Ferrel and C.R. Sanders, eds., *Cultural Criminology*, pp. 297–326. Boston: Northeastern University Press.

Foster, Mark E. 1983. "Analysis of the Newly Amended Commercial Code of Japan." *Case Western Journal of International Law* 15: 587–600.

Fukushima, Masao. 1991. "The Significance of the Enforcement of the Company Law Chapters of the Old Commercial Code in 1893." *Law in Japan* 24: 171–94.

Goffman, Erving. 1969. *Where the Action Is*. London: Penguin Press.

Hadley, Eleanor M. 1970. *Antitrust in Japan*. Princeton: Princeton University Press.

Haley, John O. 1982. "Sheathing the Sword of Justice in Japan: An Essay on Law Without Sanctions." *Journal of Japanese Studies* 8, no. 12: 265–81.

Havens, T. R. 1987. *Fire Across the Sea: The Vietnam War and Japan 1965–1975*. Princeton: Princeton University Press.

Ihara, Keiko, and Taro Hamada. 1994. "Daijobuka–Eguzekuteibu no kikiseiri" (Are you alright? Executive crisis management). *Aera*, March 14: 69.

Inaba, Takeo. 1976. "Kaishaho kaisei ni kan suru kakukai no iken ni tsuite" (Concerning various opinions regarding Commercial Code reform). *Jurisuto* 616: 21–34.

Inoue, Toru. 1966. "Kaisha–Kabunushi–Sokaiya: Sokaiya no anyaku wo yurusumono" (Companies–shareholders–*sokaiya*: Those who permit the secret maneuvers of *sokaiya*). *Jurisuto* 340: 58–61.

Isaacs, Jonathan, and Takashi Ejiri. 1990. *Japanese Securities Markets*. London: Euromoney Publications.

Ito, Tsukasa. 1996. "Sokaiya no jissai to sono boshi taisaku ni tsuite" (The actual circumstances of *sokaiya* and countermeasurers for their prevention). *Jurisuto* 340: 50–57.

"Ito-Yokado rieki yokyo jiken saiketsu" (Court decision on the demands for payoffs in the Ito-Yokado case). 1993. *Shiryopan shoji homu* 111: 83–91.

"Ito-Yokado shacho jinin" (Ito-Yokado's president resigns). 1992. *Asahi shimbun* (Tokyo), October 30: 9.

Iwai, Hiroaki. 1974. "Delinquent Groups and Organized Crime." In T. Lebra Takie, ed., *Japanese Culture and Behavior: Selected Readings*, pp. 383–95. Honolulu: University of Hawaii Press.

Japan Company Handbook. 1988. Tokyo: Toyo keizai.

———. 1994. First section (Autumn). Tokyo: Toyo keizai.

"Kabunushi sokai gaikyo—Ichigatsu sokai" (General situation of shareholder meetings: January general meetings). 1992. *Shiryopan shoji homu* 95: 149–52.

"Kabunushi sokai gaikyo—Ichigatsu sokai" (General situation of shareholder meetings: January general meetings). 1993. *Shiryopan shoji homu* 107: 89–92.

"Kabunushi sokai gaikyo—Ichigatsu sokai" (General situation of shareholder meetings: January general meetings). 1994. *Shiryopan shoji homu* 119: 207–10.

Kamesaka, Tsunesaburo. 1926. *Who's Who in Japan.* Tokyo: The Who's Who in Japan Publishing Office.

"Kanagawa-Kenkatsu, sokaiya nado ni kan suru jittai chosa matomeru: Kibokyokaiin gojyu-sha no kaito" (Kanagawa prefecture police complete results of survey concerning *sokaiya*: Answers from fifty companies in corporate protection association). 1979. *Shoji homu* 829 (25 February): 40–41.

Kanda, Toyoharu. 1991. *Sokaiya hyakunen.* Tokyo: Richmond K. K.

Kaplan, David E., and Alec Dubro. 1986. *Yakuza: The Explosive Account of Japan's Criminal Underworld.* Reading, MA: Addison Wesley.

Katzenstein, Peter J., and Yutaka Tsujinaka. 1991. *Defending the Japanese State: Structures, Norms and the Political Responses to Terrorism and Violent Social Protest in the 1970s and 1980s.* Ithaca: Cornell University East Asia Program.

Kawamoto, Ichiro. 1979a. "Kabunushi sokai no genjo to hokaisei no hitsuyo" (The present state of the general meeting of shareholders and the need for legal revision). *Hogaku semina* 6: 64–67.

———. 1979b. "Sokaiya no shikingen" (*Sokaiya* funding sources). *Hogaku semina* 8: 90–93.

Kawamoto, Ichiro, and Ittoku Monma 1976. "*Sokaiya* in Japan." *Hong Kong Law Journal* 6, no. 2: 179–88.

Kawamoto, Ichiro, Masao Kshida, Akira Morita, and Yasuhiro Kawaguchi. 1993. *Nihon no kaishaho* (The Commercial Code of Japan). Tokyo: Commercial Law Center.

Kawauchi, Toshihito. 1993. *Kigyo to dowa mondai* (Companies and the discrimination problem). Tokyo: Akashi shoten.

Keibi jitsumu kenkyukai-cho (KJK). 1989. *Uyoku undo ishiki to kodo* (Right-wing movement thought and trends). Tokyo: Tachibana shobo.

Keisatsucho boryokudan taisakuho kenkyukai (KBTK). 1992. *Shimin no tame no botaiho hayawakari* (Quick understanding of the violent group countermeasurers law for citizens). Tokyo: Kinzai.

"Keishicho, *sokaiya* nado ni kan suru chosa kekka matomeru: Sanjokin katto kigyo ga zoka" (National Police Agency completes results of survey concerning *sokaiya*, etc.: Firms cutting support money increase). 1980. *Shoji homu* 885 (25 October): 40–42.

"Keishicho, sokaiya ni kan suru chosa kekka wo happyo: Kigyogawa no kangaekata, tsukiai no jissai nado" (National Police Agency publishes results of survey concerning *sokaiya*: Corporation's ways of, thinking, circumstances of association with *sokaiya*, etc.). 1978. *Shoji homu* 815 (25 September): 36–37.

Kennedy, Dennis J., and James O. Finckenauer. 1995. *Organized Crime in America*. Belmont, CA: Wadsworth.

Kester, W. Carl. 1991. *Japanese Takeovers: The Global Contest for Corporate Control*. Boston: Harvard Business School.

Keynes, John Maynard. 1932. *Essays in Persuasion*. New York: Harcourt, Brace, and Company.

Krauss, Ellis, Thomas Rohlen, and Patricia Steinhoff. 1984. *Conflict in Japan*. Honolulu: University of Hawaii Press.

Kubo, Yuzaburo. 1964. *Sokaiya gojyunen* (Fifty years of *sokaiya*). Osaka: Hyoron shimbunsha.

Lyman, Stamford M., and Marvin B. Scott. 1968. "Coolness in Everyday Life." In M. Truzzi, ed., *Sociology and Everyday Life*, pp. 92–101. Englewood Cliffs, NJ: Prentice Hall.

Mae, Hidemitsuo. 1977. "Kigyo ni okeru sokaiya taisaku no seika ni tsuite" (Concerning the results of anti-*sokaiya* countermeasures among companies)." *Shoji homu* 771: 34–35.

Maeda, Shinjiro. 1968. *Kaisha hanzai no kenkyu* (Research on company crimes). Tokyo: Yuhikaku.

Mainichi shimbun. 1992. *Soshiki boryoku wo ou* (On the trail of organized violence). Tokyo: Mainichi shimbun.

————1994. "Sokaiya no chosen ni kusuruna" (Don't give in to the *sokaiya* challenge). *Mainichi shimbun* (June 27): 5.

McKean, Margaret A. 1981. *Environmental Protest and Citizen Politics in Japan.* Berkeley: University of California Press.

Miller, Gale. 1978. *Odd Jobs: The World of Deviant Work.* Englewood Cliffs, NJ: Prentice Hall.

Mills, C. Wright 1959. *The Sociological Imagination.* London: Oxford University Press.

Minato, Ippei. 1979. *Burakku kyapitaruizumu: Sokaiya no seitaigaku* (Black capitalism: The facts of life about *sokaiya*). Tokyo: Koron shuppan.

Mitooka, Michio. 1967. "Toyo denki kara terebi jiken no aramashi" (An outline of the Toyo electric television incident). *Gekkan shoji homu* 434: 2–3.

Miyazawa, Setsuo. 1991. "The Private Sector and Law Enforcement in Japan." In W.T. Gormley, ed., *Privatization and Its Alternatives*, pp. 241–57. Madison: University of Wisconsin Press.

Mizoguchi, Atsushi. 1993. *Gendai yakuza no ura chishiki* (Behind the scenes knowledge of modern yakuza). Tokyo: Nihon purintekusu.

Motoki, Shin, Takeo Kosugi, and William D. Johnson 1981. "Explanation of the Amended Stock Corporation Law." *The Japan Business Law Journal* 2, no. 8: 309–54.

Nakabayashi, Eiji. 1978. "Sokaiya no doko to taisakujo no shomondai" (*Sokaiya* trends and various countermeasure problems). *Soji homu* 803: 655–58.

National Police Agency (NPA). 1978. *Keisatsu hakusho, 1978* (Police white paper, 1978). Tokyo: Okurasho insatsukyoku.

————. 1979. *Keisatsu hakusho, 1979* (Police white paper, 1979). Tokyo: Okurasho insatsukyoku.

————. 1982. *Keisatsu hakusho, 1982* (Police white paper, 1982). Tokyo: Okurasho insatsukyoku.

————. 1983. *Keisatsu hakusho, 1983* (Police white paper, 1983). Tokyo: Okurasho insatsukyoku.

————. 1986. *Keisatsu hakusho, 1986* (Police white paper, 1986). Tokyo: Okurasho insatsukyoku.

————. 1988. *Keisatsu hakusho, 1988* (Police white paper, 1986). Tokyo: Okurasho insatsukyoku.

————. 1989. *Keisatsu hakusho, 1989* (Police white paper, 1989). Tokyo: Okurasho insatsukyoku.

Nihon Bengoshi Rengokai. 1986. *Minji kainyu boryoku* (Violent intervention in civil affairs). Tokyo: Commercial Law Center.

Noguchi, Yukio. 1994. "Closing the Books on the Bubble Years." *Japan Echo* 21 (special issue): 8–18.

O'Donnell, Patrick. 1981. "Bank America's New Chief Expects Profits to Remain Depressed During Near Term," *Wall Street Journal*, April 22: 4.

Okumura, Hiroshi. 1986. *Nihon no kabushiki kaisha* (Japanese corporations). Tokyo: Toyo keizai shimposha.

————. 1992. "Corporate Capitalism: Cracks in the System." *Japan Quarterly* 39, no. 1: 54–61.

Okushima, Takayasu. 1981. "Commercial Law." *Waseda Bulletin of Comparative Law* 1: 38–41.

Okushima, Takayasu, and Yasuhiko Nose. 1982. "Commercial Law." *Waseda Bulletin of Comparative Law* 2: 89–92.

Okushima, Takayasu. and Yasuhiko Yamada. 1983. "Commercial Law." *Waseda Bulletin of Comparative Law* 3: 121–29.

Osumi, Tatsuo. 1966. *Kabunushi sokai unei no jitsumu to homu* (The administrative and legal management of shareholder meetings). Tokyo: Jiyu kokuminsha.

————.1971. "Kabunushi sokai seijoka e no michi" (The road to shareholder meeting normalcy). *Asahi shimbun*, May 29: 9.

Passin, Herbert. 1975. "Intellectuals in the Decision-Making Process." In E.F. Vogel, ed., *Modern Japanese Organization and Decision-making*, 251–83. Berkeley: University of California Press.

Pharr, Susan J. 1990. *Losing Face: Status Politics in Japan*. Berkeley: University of California Press.

Rengo Press. 1965. *The Japan Biographical Encyclopedia and Who's Who*. Tokyo: Rengo Press.

Repeta, Lawrence. 1988. "Declining Public Ownership of Japanese Industry: A Case of Regulatory Failure?" In J.O. Haley, ed., *Law and Society in Contemporary Japan: American Perspectives*, pp. 113–38. Dubuque: Kendall/Hunt.

Report of the Mission on Japanese Combines (RMJC). 1946. *Corporation Law and the Zaibatsu Problem*. Report to the Department of State, part 1 (March).

Rubner, Alex. 1965. *The Ensnared Shareholder: Directors and the Modern Corporation*. New York: St. Martin's Press.

Rustin, Richard E., and Masayoshi Kanabayashi. 1981. "Japan Exports Ways to Quiet Shareholders." *Wall Street Journal*, 16 April 29: 40.

Salwin, Lester N. 1962. "The New Commercial Code of Japan: Symbol of Gradual Progress Toward Democratic Goals." *Georgetown Law Journal* 50: 478–512.

"Shinkaisha setsuritsu ni himerareta nazo" (The secret enigma of the establishment of a new company). 1994. *Shukan toyo keizai*, 12 March: 38 (New York).

Shiso undo kenkyujo. 1972. *Sayoku hyaku shudan* (100 left-wing groups). Tokyo: Mizushima tsuyoshi K. K.

"Showa 56–nen kaisha ho kaisei no seiritsu" (The formation of the 1982 Commercial Code amendment). *Jurisuto* 747: 22–26.

Smith, Malcolm D. H., and Hiroshi Tamiya. 1978. "Comment: Commercial Law Reform in Japan: The Current Debate." *Law in Japan* 11: 102–11.

"Sokaiya no mitsuida kigyo 240–sha risuto" (List of 240 companies Financing *Sokaiya*). 1978b. *Shukan daiyamondo*, 10 June: 120–25.

"Sokaiya to kigyo no tantosha no daienkai." (A large banquet for *sokaiya* and corporation managers). 1991. *Asahi shimbun* (Tokyo), June 22: 9.

"Sokaiya to no yuchaku wo kotonare (Refuse ties to *sokaiya*). 1993. *Nihon keizai shimbun*, 15 July: 2.

Stille, Alexander. 1995. *Excellent Cadavers: The Mafia and the Death of the First Italian Republic*. New York: Pantheon Books.

Suzuki, Kunio. 1993 *Datsu uyoku sengen* (Escape the right manifesto). Tokyo: IPC. Suzuki, Takeo. 1981.

Szymkowiak, Kenneth F., and Patricia Steinhoff. "Wrapping Up in Something Long: Intimidation and Violence by Right-Wing Groups in Postwar Japan." *Terrorism and Political Violence* 7, no. 1: 265–98.

Takagi Masyuki. 1989. *Uyoku–Katsudo to dantai* (The right wing: Activities and groups). Tokoyo: Doyo bijitsusha.

Taniguchi, Shoichi. 1980. "Jitsumu no kokore" (Understanding of business affairs). In K. Ariyama, ed., *Shareholder Meetings and Corporate Defense Associations*, 536–60. Osaka: Ariyama Trade Service.

Taniguchi, Tomohiko. 1993. *Japan's Banks and the "Bubble Economy" of the Late 1980s*. Princeton: Center for International Studies.

Uekusa, Kazuhide. 1991. "The Making and Breaking of a Bubble Economy." *Japan Echo* 18, no. 4: 23–27.

Upham, Frank. 1987. *Law and Social Change in Postwar Japan*. New York: Alfred A. Knopf.

Van Wolferen, Karel. 1989. *The Enigma of Japanese Power*. New York: Albert A. Knopf.

Violent Group Countermeasures (VGC) (1994). "Sokaiya taisaku ni tsuite" (Concerning *sokaiya* countermeasures). Unpublished.

West, Mark D. 1999. "Information, Institutions, and Extortion in Japan and the United States: Making Sense of *Sokaiya* Racketeers." *Northwestern University Law Review* 93, no. 3: 767–817.

Wood Christopher. 1992. *The Bubble Economy: Japan's Extraordinary Speculative Boom of the '80s and the Dramatic Bust of the '90s*. New York: Atlantic Monthly Press.

Yamamura, Kozu. 1967. *Economic Policy in Postwar Japan*. Berkeley: University of California Press.

Yazawa Atsushi, Hoshino Takashi, Takeuchi Akio, and Kitazawa Masanori. 1975. "Kaishaho no komponteki kaisei no mondaiten" (Problems of the fundamental reform of the Commercial Code). *Jurisuto* 593: 14–38.

"Zoka suru Boryoku-sokaiya no gokuhi risuto o hatsukokai" (Publication of the secret list of increasingly violent *sokaiya*). 1978. *Shukan daiyamondo*, 27 May: 82–85.

Index

Crime *(continued)*
  murder, of Suzuki, 3–4, 155,
    166–171
  See also Sokaiya
Crime syndicates. *See*
    Organized-crime groups

D

Dai-Ichi Kangyo Bank, 174
Daiwa Securities, 124, 174
Dark Ocean Society, 44
DeVos, George, 44
Dow Chemical, 107
Drucker, Peter F., 47

E

East Asia Comrades Association, 62
Eastern Precinct Enterprise
    Protection Association, 80
Economy, 21, 156–160
Edwards, Corwin D., 46, 49
Eisenhower, Dwight, 61
Ejiri, Takashi, 9
Enkaiya (adjourners), 15
Enshutsuya (producers), 15
Exchange rate, 157
Extortion crimes, 154, 163–164
  See also Sokaiya

F

Falcone, Giovanni, xiii
Ferrel, Jeff, 7
Finckenauer, James O., 4, 163
First Chicago, 107
Foreign firms, *sokaiya* contact
    with, 107–108
Foreign shareholders, 170
Foster, Mark E., 99–100, 101
Fuji Fire and Marine Insurance
    Company, 123

Fuji Photo Film, xi, 155, 166–167
Fukao, Ryutaro, 39–40
Fukushima, Masao, 35
Furui, Yoshimi, 98, 101–102

G

General Motors, 107
Gilbert, Lewis and John, 131
Go, Seinosuke, 38
Goffman, Erving, 130
Goto, Keita, 54
Greenmailer (*shite*) groups, 9
Gross domestic product (GDP), 157
Group structure, 22–23, 24–26

H

Hadley, Eleanor M., 49
Haley, John O., 69
Hanai, Takuzo, 37, 53
Hattori, Takeshi, 65
Havens, T.R., 72
Heiwado Company, 123
Heiwa Sogo Bank, 114
Hiroshima Group, 64, 74
Hoikusei-kai, 62
Holding Company Liquidation
    Committee (HCLC), 50
Hotel New Japan scandal, 53

I

Inaba, Takeo, 97
Inamoto, Toruo, 113
Inoue, Kichigoro, 38
Inoue, Toru, 9
Interest rates, 157
Intermediaries
  in civil disputes, 161, 164–165
  at shareholder meetings, 14
International Business Machines
    (IBM), 107

Kenneth F. Szymkowiak from Temple University received his bachelor's degree in journalism in 1975 from Temple University. He worked as a reporter and editor in the Philadelphia area until 1980, when he worked as a general assignment reporter for the *Miami News*. In 1982 he received a Gannett Fellowship and spent a year studying Asian issues at the University of Hawaii-Manoa. This was followed by a five-year stay in Japan as a freelance journalist. He returned to the United States in 1988 and a year later began graduate school at the University of Hawaii in sociology. He received a Fulbright Fellowship in 1993 supporting eighteen months of research in Japan on *sokaiya*. He received his doctorate in sociology in 1996 from the University of Hawaii at Honolulu. At present, he is teaching and conducting research in Honolulu.